90   D1343285

Praise for **RACE MANNERS**

"An enlightening and balanced view of racial conflict. Jacobs deftly defuses explosive scenarios by offering alternative interpretations and by dispensing sensitive advice to both sides. A primer for understanding another person's point of view on the issues of race, *Race Manners* is a 'must read' for those who wish to clarify racial dilemmas."
—Norine Dresser, *Los Angeles Times* columnist

"*Race Manners* advances racial understanding. It provides the clearest road map for what each of us can do to lower suspicion by examining how our own preconceptions lead to actions which block meaningful dialogue. . . . A call to extraordinary action." —*Raleigh News & Observer*

"With a journalist's eye and a poet's ear, Jacobs acknowledges and examines the complexities behind all types of racially charged encounters. He insightfully points out rational and irrational behaviors, suggests reasons for them, and makes common-sense suggestions to ease the reader out of many racial quagmires. . . . A rare exception, a book that unflinchingly looks at even the most mundane aspects of racism and offers practical advice to counter its insidious effects." —*Baltimore City Paper*

"Jacobs's book has shown up right on time. *Race Manners* is a guided tour through the perspectives that have become arguments that have come to compete for our passions in the discussion of race relations in this country. . . . He boldly excavates racial dilemmas from the long record of socioeconomic inequality, the broad concept of personal respect, and the delicate brushstrokes of cross-cultural etiquette."
—*OC Weekly*

"A guidebook for Americans on how to think constructively about race . . . Eloquent . . . Wise." —*Arizona Republic*

"Required reading . . . *Race Manners* could generate the kinds of questions that could change American history." —*Springfield Republican*

"The best book I have read on American race relations." —Bob Koch, WXXI-FM, Rochester

"An impressive contribution that exposes the underlying silliness as well as noxiousness of American racial attitudes." —*Kirkus Reviews*

"A frank, intelligent guide intended for both whites and blacks . . . Jacobs challenges preconceptions and entrenched myths." —*Publishers Weekly*

"Since first discovering *Race Manners*, I have recommended it to clients all over the nation. The feedback was universally positive and came from the highest levels of diversity leadership." —Sondra Thiederman, consultant and author of *Making Diversity Work*

RACE MANNERS

RACE MANNERS

NAVIGATING THE MINEFIELD BETWEEN BLACK AND WHITE AMERICANS

BRUCE A. JACOBS

Arcade Publishing
New York

Copyright © 1999, 2006, 2011 by Bruce A. Jacobs

All Rights Reserved. No part of this book may be reproduced in any manner without the express written consent of the publisher, except in the case of brief excerpts in critical reviews or articles. All inquiries should be addressed to Arcade Publishing, 307 West 36th Street, 11th Floor, New York, NY 10018.

Arcade Publishing books may be purchased in bulk at special discounts for sales promotion, corporate gifts, fund-raising, or educational purposes. Special editions can also be created to specifications. For details, contact the Special Sales Department, Arcade Publishing, 307 West 36th Street, 11th Floor, New York, NY 10018 or info@skyhorsepublishing.com.

Arcade Publishing® is a registered trademark of Skyhorse Publishing, Inc.®, a Delaware corporation.

Visit our website at www.arcadepub.com.

10 9 8 7 6 5 4 3 2 1

Library of Congress Cataloging-in-Publication Data

Jacobs, Bruce A.
   Race manners : navigating the minefield between black and white Americans / Bruce A. Jacobs.
      p. cm.
   ISBN 978-1-61145-031-6 (pbk. : alk. paper)
   1. United States--Race relations. 2. African Americans--Life skills guides. 3. Whites--United States--Life skills guides. I. Title.
   E185.615.J297 2011
   305.800973--dc22

2011001759

Printed in the United States of America

For my mother and father,
who gave me this life

To expand the universe
one pushes out
the plate glass windows.

—Stephen Jonas, 1961

If you see yourself in others
then who can you harm?

—Buddha

CONTENTS

IDENTITY

JUST BETWEEN US

RACE MANNERS
FOR THE 21ST CENTURY

Introduction

"Shut Up!": Fear, Trash Talk, and the Death of Discourse

*"S*hut up!
"*Yeah, I'm talking to you, you ignorant slime. You traitor. With ideas like yours, you don't even deserve to be an American. You people don't have a clue. Why don't you just go sign up with the enemy? Yeah. You scum-sucking rodent. You dumb-as-mud specimen. Why don't you just SHUT UP!"*

Welcome to the new American conversation. How are you liking it so far?

If you're not with us, you're against us. If you don't get your way, you're a victim of persecution. If you challenge official wisdom, you're told to watch what you say.

1

And if you dare to call in and challenge the choreographed tirades of any of the barking attack hosts who now dominate much of radio and TV opinion programming, you're set up as fodder for ridicule by an audience drunk on derision and scorn.

Call it the profit-driven trivialization of news and discourse. Our nation is engulfed in it as never before. And in spite of the sheer volume of our outpourings of verbosity, our actual understanding of one another — as peoples of different colors, orientations, and beliefs who share a nation and a planet — is poorer than ever.

How did we get to this? And how can we get out of it?

I suggest that what we are now caught up in, in all of its small-minded fury, is the personalizing of political and cultural difference. We have cheapened our measure of public discourse to the point where our disagreements and conflicts register more as mere attacks on one another than as substantial challenges to one another's ideas and actions.

There is a method to the madness. For the centralized corporate news operations that now dominate the industry, it is more profitable to have mediocre reporters covering car crashes and passively repeating accusations, and talk show guests shouting at one another on cardboard sets in the studio, than it is to send good reporters out to dig up important stories and to have well-informed guests in the studio engaging in respectful debate. So, for the sake of profit and cheap dramatic impact, news operations have dialed back the pursuit of actual journalism. Instead, the people who read the news to us and who hold forth on talk shows have heightened the personal, "entertaining" aspect of politics. Reporters tend to highlight personal scandal, matters of campaign style, charisma, who got in the best licks in a debate — a sort of sports-coverage form of political reporting. And for the pundits, the coveted coin of today's realm is anger: shouting, interrupting, mocking, sneering. It's all about the show.

Meanwhile, the ideas and principles we are supposed to be fighting about — our actual reasons for caring in the first place — are sucked out of the conversation. What is left is rude, crude, shallow attacking and counterattacking. Most of us claim to dislike it. But we watch and listen to it anyway.

We all know what this spectacle of empty spite has done to our national politics. But how often do we think about the damage it has done to each of us personally when it comes to dealing with issues of real contention in our daily lives?

Here is where it hits home: *Our being hammered through our TVs and car radios by this steady wave of petty warfare succeeds, often without our knowing it, in boxing our issues of social disagreement into the socially taboo category of personal attack.* So when it comes to our real everyday disagreements with people we know over matters of politics or race or culture, we feel we have nowhere to go. We feel as if we have only two options: to attack one another's very personhood, or to shut down. Those are our received choices: get abusively in-your-face with those who disagree with us and tell them to shut up, or shut up ourselves so that we can retreat to bitterly commiserate with those who agree with us.

The idea behind the "Shut up!" approach — it's an epithet favored by the meanest of today's talk show hosts as a way to cut off callers and guests who are on the "wrong" side of an issue — seems to have now become the dominant ethic of popular political discourse in the United States. This idea, the idea that political struggle is all about personal abuse, has served to shut down every one of us at one time or another when it comes to saying the political things we most need to say in daily life: How we are angry, or how we are perplexed, or how we are up in arms about some social or cultural or political or racial event in our lives.

The things we most desperately need to say to one another to address our problems do not get said because *the verbally violent talk-show-assassin style of conversation to which we have become publicly accustomed is not permissible in everyday life.* Even if it does work as entertainment, giving us a vicarious thrill by letting media personalities in effect talk dirty for us, it never, ever works in real life, and talking that way is not allowed in any civilized household or classroom or workplace, and we know it. Plus, it can get you punched in the mouth, or worse. Even those of us who enjoy the bigmouthed bully shows still realize that we cannot talk that way to people in the real world and get away with it. A person can only talk that way when protected by a microphone, a TV camera, or bodyguards.

So where does that leave you and me? Where does that leave us when, after we turn off the TV or the radio, we come face-to-face in real life with a person of another race or another religion or another sexual orientation who says or does or believes something that we have trouble dealing with? It leaves us to make a desperate choice: shut up or shut them up.

That isn't good enough.

Shutting up — and shutting other people up — is no way for any of us to live in a world full of different kinds of people. It won't work. And it will leave you feeling even more under siege, and knowing even less, than before.

This updated version of *Race Manners* will give you some better options.

In my travels speaking across the country in the years since the release of the first edition of *Race Manners*, I have heard person after person — people who often disagree with one another on major issues of race or politics — fervently wish aloud for some way to cut through the public verbal gunfire in order to actually be understood. Since the September 11, 2001, attacks and the ensuing lockdown of national opinion, fear and loathing of the cultural and political "other" has ratcheted up to excruciatingly new levels. A young white woman in a far western state told me how she had to sneak *Race Manners* into her house and hide the book from her parents — and how shocked and relieved she was to learn that it is possible to confront deep racial biases in oneself and others without the savage-or-be-savaged ritual of personal abuse. A young black man at an East Coast college told me of his constant frustration with the inability to simply be seen as who he is rather than as a poster child for the latest media images of black youth. A white farmer in West Virginia told me he thinks it's high time for both rural and urban people to realize how we all suffer from the damage done by narrow, corporate-dominated news coverage; his particular complaint was about the activities of giant agribusiness companies and their effect on his livelihood. An Iranian American woman in Baltimore told me bluntly that she has virtually stopped traveling because she can no longer stand the humiliation of being constantly pulled out of lines and treated as a suspect at airports.

I decided to offer this new version of *Race Manners* to help us to deal sanely and constructively with the world in which we now find ourselves: a world after September 11, one riddled with fears and slogans, a society in which the explosion of talk show culture has made American political discourse largely an industry of personal warfare. At the same time, I saw a need to update the book's discussion of many of the ongoing racial questions that Americans, particularly blacks and whites, continue to face in everyday life. In this new edition, I broaden the conversation further beyond black and white than in the first edition, but I also focus in places on issues in which blacks and whites have specific history. As before, to the extent that we as Americans of all ethnicities and backgrounds have shared experiences, this book is for all of us.

In this updated *Race Manners,* you'll find a new chapter on how to survive today's contagiously mean radio and TV talk show state of mind. You'll find new chapters on dealing with your own fears of terrorism in your travels; seeing how American black/white relations play into attitudes toward Muslims and peoples of Arab descent; understanding what the concept of race means, and what it doesn't mean, now that scientific research is finding race to be physiologically meaningless; deciding whether and when it is worth it for you to speak up among friends, family, or coworkers on a difficult or dangerous issue; and looking beyond the facile notion of "tolerance" to see a deeper way of appreciating one another, as well as other new and continuing issues in our daily struggle for informed coexistence. Nearly every chapter of this new

Race Manners concludes with a set of what I call "Survival Suggestions": potent, assertive ways to handle issues in a manner that serves both sanity and fairness.

I intend for this new version of *Race Manners* to give you contemporary tools for living out an old axiom: People tend to want to speak as they are spoken to, and to listen as they are listened to. I want this book to serve as a reassurance of the kinds of political and personal interchange and growth we might share with friends and neighbors and coworkers, and also as a warning of how that potential is now being denied us by a climate that continually compels us to be afraid — of one another, of "them," of the unknown — and to be contemptuous of all except what we think we know. I hope that this book will help you to anchor the day-to-day doings of your life in the knowledge that democracy — a word now much repeated but little heeded — is much more about disagreement than it is about head-nodding unanimity. Democracy is much more about entertaining protest than it is about forbidding or punishing it. It is much more about difference than it is about agreement.

In that sense, I want *Race Manners* to serve you as a kind of personal handbook for defending your own piece of democracy against a storm-trooper ethic that seeks to crush true discussion and dissent. The fact is, we are all under a tremendous amount of pressure right now to act as paranoid recruits for lockstep thinking rather than as healthy citizens. We are under pressure to not become well informed about those with whom we share the world. We are under pressure to ignore or annihilate the viewpoints of other Americans who disagree with us. We are under pressure to keep our mouths shut in public — unless we repeat a party line — and to instead let media hit men do our talking for us.

Don't cave in under the pressure. Stand up and use your voice.

This new edition of *Race Manners* will help to show you how.

Out in the Open

1

Black, White, and Scared: Our New Scapegoating in the Post-9/11 Age

S eptember 11, 2001. The twin towers fall. Nearly three thousand people die. Americans stand, shocked, in front of television sets in department stores and waiting rooms and offices, watching two jetliners bury themselves in the upper floors of New York's most iconic skyscrapers, where they explode into fireballs. They watch office workers dive to their deaths from nearly 100 stories aloft as the inferno grows. They watch the presumably immutable twin symbols of American capitalism disintegrate in an apocalyptic torrent of concrete and steel and ash.

The social messages begin right away. Major news programs begin emblazoning their sets with slogans such as

"America under Attack." Reporters begin wearing American flags on their lapels on camera. The formerly little recognized Osama bin Laden and Al-Qaeda, the apparent perpetrators of the attack, instantly become household names. The president goes on television to declare bin Laden a fugitive wanted "dead or alive" in a "War on Terror." Airport security becomes an ugly combination of personal screening and profiling. Hearing color-coded government bulletins of the current terrorism risk becomes routine. All Americans are effectively deputized to watch for "suspicious" persons or activities. The entire nation is declared a danger zone.

Suddenly, being an Arab American — or someone mistaken for an Arab American — in an airport or on a plane seems to become grounds for questioning and search by authorities and for general scrutiny by other passengers. Nervous glances at presumed Arab Americans or Muslims become commonplace. The fearful watchfulness spreads to all public places. Assaults against Arab Americans and desecrations of American mosques increase. So does the social permissibility of virulently anti-Arab cartoons, jokes, and on-air remarks. Respectable people denounce such behavior. But everyone seems to agree that 9/11 has created a new set of American attitudes out of whole cloth.

It's a new world, say the pundits after 9/11. Everything has changed.

Or has it?

If there is one twisted quip that says it all about blacks, whites, and race since 9/11, I think it is what a friend of mine overheard a black person say in the thick of the anti-

Arab hysteria following the Twin Towers attacks: "Finally! Somebody besides us for white people to be afraid of."

Forget the claims about "everything being different" and its being "a whole new world" since the attacks on the World Trade Center. Perhaps Americans drink from a new cauldron, but it overflows with the same old poison: persistent fear of ethnic retribution, and the casualties thereof.

It began with what one might call the original American reign of terror: the bloody conquest of this continent and the awful hold it maintains over the national psyche. White Americans, for their part, have been chronically afraid since at least the sixteenth century, when European settlers began a fouled coexistence with the peoples whose lands they would inexorably take by force. The collective white fright swelled with the fallout from the successive white-ruled regimes of African slavery, lynch law, and Jim Crow, and has since been sustained by the working and middle classes' ongoing dread of the black urban poor. Take a look at the emotional planks of any national Republican political campaign since the infamous Willie Horton ad of 1988 — in which clever Republican strategists for George H. W. Bush used the image of an escaped black rapist to stir white fears about the Democratic welfare state — and you will see the legacy confirmed. If there is a trait embedded even more deeply in the mainstream American character than the pursuit of money, it is fear of the Other. It is at the very heart of the way the dominant American culture learned to view the new world it had conquered. How could it be otherwise? When a society is layered, century after century, atop the fractured foundation of unmitigated conquest and unanswered rage, a perpetual state of unease and fear is assured.

So fear is what we've got. One of the best, and most cruelly funny, portrayals of this can be found partway through Michael Moore's film *Bowling for Columbine*, in a satirical *South Park*–style cartoon sequence purporting to provide a capsule version of American history. The sequence is a series of historical scenes in which whites abuse successive populations of peoples of color — Indians, then blacks, and so on — whose survivors then loom menacingly in the background while the whites huddle terrified in a circle, eyes wide and teeth chattering. If you haven't seen it, do. In addition to being funny, it is a ruthlessly vivid illustration of how paranoia, over a period of centuries, becomes lodged in the national personality.

And there it remains. There exists, today, a broad swath of white Americans, particularly the economically insecure, who continue to anchor their self-images in fear and suppression of the Other, as if fearfully looking back over their shoulders at history's throngs of wronged and angry nonwhite peoples — in particular, at Native Americans and the descendants of imported Africans — while trying to outrun their own panicky sense of being stalked from behind. There is no getting around it: when one has seized a continent through genocide, enslavement, and broken treaties and has never circled back to make things right, it is hard to so much as move a muscle without watching one's back. There is no inner moral peace under such conditions. There is no quiet internal sense of rightness. Which is why, today, the American flag is waved so wildly and the anthems are screamed with such abandon.

And so, from the antebellum whites drunk on legends about bloodthirsty oversexed Africans to today's unemployed white guys mesmerized by radio rants about Muslims, a certain number of jittery, precariously footed white Americans have perpetually defined themselves according to their fear and loathing of others. They leap to embrace contempt for the other with the kind of desperation that only a fleeing person can muster. They feel the scourge of collective culpability at their backs, breathing heavily. And so they run, losing themselves in a rush of righteous rage, as if an escape from conscience could ever be possible.

Those Americans targeted by this long-running fear and loathing are, naturally, angry about it. Blacks are angry about being indiscriminately feared on the street and overlooked in city hall and Washington. Latinos are angry about being stereotyped and economically marginalized. Native Americans are angry about having their land stolen and their peoples and traditions nearly (or in some cases wholly) exterminated. Women are angry about being denied full partnership and equal rewards in society. Jews are angry about being mocked and defamed and having their history, including the Holocaust, denied or sugarcoated. Gays are angry about having their very existence defined as sinful and their civil and human rights denied. Asian Americans are angry about being culturally caricatured and treated as if they have no grievances a mere sixty years after the Japanese American internment camps.

And many Arab Americans, for their part, are angry about being feared and fingered as the latest "them" in a four-hundred-year-old string of official national bogeymen.

There has been an increase in American hate crimes against Muslims, among them attacks upon mosques and personal assaults. President George W. Bush broadly included portions of the Arab world as part of the so-called Axis of Evil, and his administration undertook unprecedented surveillance and detention of Muslims and people of Arab descent, often in secret and without due process, on the grounds of alleged ties to terrorism. A series of inflammatory Danish cartoons (one of which pictured the prophet Muhammad with a turban shaped like a bomb) infuriated Muslims; in the wake of the West's subsequent insensitivity to the offensiveness of the cartoons, years of Muslim anger worldwide exploded into violence. Right-wing commentators have made outlandish anti-Arab remarks, such as Ann Coulter's that the United States should "invade their countries, kill their leaders, and convert them to Christianity,"[1] which got her fired as a columnist for the *National Review.* Many Americans feel free to make insulting and stereotypical remarks about Arabs and Muslims. (I remember overhearing a white shopkeeper sarcastically refer to the Muslim holy holiday Ramadan as "Rama-dama-ding-dong." I gave her a nasty look, left the store, and have not been back since.) In response to this overall climate, the Council on American-Islamic Relations, a nonprofit Muslim advocacy group, now offers Muslims free "Know Your Rights" and "Muslim Community Safety Kit" brochures.

If you are an Arab American enraged at the slurs, the widespread intellectual laziness, the political demagoguery, and the official and unofficial abuses that create so much grief and insult and outright danger for you, I cannot pretend to offer authoritative advice. But I can offer you, along with my outrage and solidarity, an observation I have found to be true in my own life experience as a black man often targeted for suspicion: it can be both emotionally helpful and tactically useful to remind yourself of the long and demented history of the beast of American racism. The roots of the ethnic phobia displayed by that person seated next to you on the plane or in the waiting room are centuries deep, and the current version now revolving around you as an Arab American is but the latest symptom of a profound national illness whose excising demands the most radical of long-term surgeries. It is a national dysfunction of the first order, sustaining a view of others that is so rank with brutal egoism and blind selfishness that it approaches sociopathy on a collective scale. In that sense, your struggle for fairness and justice is the latest incarnation of the good fight: the reconciliation of the American psyche with the actual world. It might be helpful for you to regard it as such.

The thing for all of us to understand, then, as the black person who made the cruel quip at the beginning of this chapter knew, is that the basis for each successive new popular fear of "them" is as old as the first Thanksgiving. It is the same old doomed American attempt at escaping the wrath of the wronged. The incredible potency of 9/11, for many American whites, was the way in which it enabled them to shed their moral ambiguity in yet another fit of fear against a dark avenger. It provided a similar basis for righteous anger among many Americans of all ethnicities.

For some blacks, in particular, 9/11 supplied an additional payoff: it provided a powerful sense of relief from the age-old burden of perceived black villainy — at the expense, in this case, of peoples of Arab descent. Among some blacks, bone-tired of a lifetime of being scapegoated and dodged in public, the specter of Arab Americans as the new public enemy seemed a not unwelcome prospect. Being stigmatized gets old after a few hundred years, and for some blacks the prospect of feeling the shoe on the other foot — and using it to give another ethnic minority a swift kick — was too tempting to pass up.

But what gives the 9/11 epic its own ferocity as a narrative of the feared avenger is the brutal and intimate economic and political relationship between the United States and the poorer nations of the world, many of them heavily Muslim. We Americans remain largely shielded from the process through which our nation's fabulous wealth washes up on our shores: a system euphemistically called "free trade" that is in reality a ruthlessly coercive rule of huge Western-based corporations over the local economies of nations rich in natural resources and cheap labor. Thanks to news programming and political discourse that gloss lightly over these deep conflicts, we as Americans have a hard time seeing the ugly machinery behind the bounteous offerings at our department stores and supermarkets. According to the United Nations, the richest 20 percent of the world's population accounts for 86 percent of the world's consumption — including 45 percent of all meat and fish and 58 percent of total energy.[2] When the United States supports corrupt regimes in Asia or the Middle East or Africa or South America, and when the leaders of those regimes clamp down on their own people to create a cheap and easily controlled labor force and a ready flow of exported goods and raw materials, it is America more than any other country that gets the oil, the inexpensive patio furniture, the TVs, the sneakers, the bananas, the coffee, the computers, while the mostly brown-skinned people who generate the products have to do without democracy or decent wages or health care.

In a sense, it is Americans' very ability to choose from a hundred brand names of furniture that requires people in other parts of the world to suffer. In the brutally ruled and often economically undeveloped parts of the world from which these riches come, many of the citizens look unkindly, to say the least, upon America and the industrialized West for sustaining this arrangement. A few of these citizens are sufficiently enraged, or desperate, to respond favorably to the bloody entreaties of certain fundamentalist groups who promise revenge.

All of this provides the raw material for our nation's latest avenger scare, whereby we explode into fight-or-flight against yet another enraged seeker of vengeance while we ignore the most obvious causes and mechanisms of the rage.

Before we succumb to this foolishness any further, I suggest we ask ourselves two questions.

First, on a moral level, how can a group or a nation possibly defend its acting, collectively, like a big, self-obsessed baby on the historic question of the grievances of others? If you are a fair-minded white person, how can you justify turning a blind eye to history and yielding instead to the knee-jerk impulse of centuries' worth of self-justifying fear? If you are a self-respecting black person with any empathy whatsoever for abused peoples, how can you rationalize surrendering to the pile-on reflex of the fear-the-Arabs mob when only yesterday it was you at the bottom of the swarming horde? And if, worse, you as an African American take compensatory pleasure in your sudden new role as an Arab stomper, how do you propose to look at yourself in the mirror now that you have lowered yourself to the moral stature of a 1950s white segregationist?

And then there is the second question: Morality aside, what do you truly gain from joining in on the fear?

How does it actually benefit you? Forget ethics for a moment. Let's be selfishly practical about it. Your chance of dying in a terrorist attack in any given year is infinitesimal. But your overall chance of being murdered is 1 in 11,000, your chance of being robbed is 1 in 400, and your chance of being burglarized is 1 in 50.[3] The vast majority of crimes in America are committed by white men. So if you are white, how does it serve your safety to pour daily energy into fearing a lifelong procession of unarmed Arab-American strangers while ignoring white men? Would it not serve you better to instead support ideas and policies that will actually increase your security? And if you are black, how does it serve your self-interest for you to feed the same old cyclical national appetite for racial paranoia that will come back around to kick you in your own butt next week? No matter who you are, how does it benefit you to ignore the true problem — a massive international enmity toward America because of what we do with other nations' economies and governments — while obsessing over the unreal problem of whether the brown-skinned person next to you on the subway is carrying explosives? Name one tangible benefit you enjoy from participating in the ongoing national frenzy of personalized fear — aside from the mean-spirited rush of flashing your self-righteous "preparedness" at a brown-skinned stranger while your own government continues to further endanger you.

This is madness, and it is hurting you and me, and we need to stop it.

To be sure, it can be difficult and unpopular and even unsafe, in some quarters, to challenge ourselves and our friends and loved ones and neighbors and coworkers at a time when a preoccupying paranoia carries the respectability of network television and radio commentary. But so what? When has it ever been easy to buck the blanketing certainty of current convention in favor of the longer view of what is right? When has it ever been easy to insist that we as a community do what actually works instead of simply stoking the self-defeating fires of popular fascination?

It was not easy for those who spoke out early against the Vietnam War — among them the Reverend Martin Luther King and linguist and activist Noam Chomsky — to do so in the face of an arrogant American military and a war-sympathetic public. Nor was it easy for those, again including Chomsky, who opposed early plans for America's Iraq War in the face of the same obstacles. Nor, for that matter, was it easy for those who opposed the McCarthy-era anticommunist witch hunts or who stood up early for civil rights for blacks, women, and gays, respectively.

Like it or not, you and I face our own moral and practical choice right now, in the years after 9/11, as to who we intend to be in this world. This is the way history happens: with invisible, unheralded decisions by people like you and me concerning how we will think and act. Right now, at this very moment, you are part of the future, and you will be so judged by those who later look back upon our time. You might not like bearing the burden of choice. But it is yours regardless, and whether by action or inaction, your decision will shape the outcome.

So what's it going to be? A positive, adult course of action that regards others as fully human and strives for solutions through relationships in the world? Or a fearful, simplistic course that once again stigmatizes the villainous avenger while avoiding the issues that would actually solve the problem?

Whether you choose to look at it ethically or practically, there is really only one sound choice.

Survival Suggestions

1. Understand that the only "new" thing about the post-9/11 hysteria is its flavor.

Don't fall for the hype about "everything being different"; it is dead-end reasoning that leaves you at the mercy of fearmongering public figures who offer rhetoric and aggression but no true solutions. Yes, the tactics for addressing mobile, decentralized terrorists are very different from those for other types of conflicts. But the underlying solution to this newest reign of terror is the same as the solutions to our previous ones: understand and address the grievances that drive the conflict. In this case they are the Israeli occupation of Palestine, American abetting of economic and political injustice in heavily Muslim nations, and now the war in Iraq. If we fail to deal with these triggers, we will chase bands of terrorists forever.

2. Don't let any new attacks erode your power to reason.

There may yet be more attacks on American soil; there may not be. Don't let them make you lose your mind. Remember suggestion number 1: Americans' reflexively reacting to such threats with paranoia and blind self-righteousness has been drilled into the national persona for centuries. Keep your head instead, and be a part of the true solution.

3. Don't scapegoat or stereotype.

It is not only unforgivably mean, it is useless. The truly mammoth terrorism risks (see chapter 3) have almost nothing to do with the brown-skinned person beside you on the plane or in the subway. If you are a person of color mistreating others in this way, or taking pleasure in there now being other targets besides you, you ought to be ashamed. Quit it. Soon enough, that hammer is going to come down on you.

4. If you are scapegoated, take care of yourself, but know as well that you are dealing with a sick culture.

As I have said, so many Americans are accustomed to hyping mythologized avengers that the illness is as reflexive to them as sneezing. If you are targeted for scrutiny or abuse, do all you need to do to defend yourself: protest, organize, sue, whatever. But try not to be burdened by the belief that this is a new form of abuse. It's not. And as you know, it's not about you at all.

5. Speak to others across lines of fear.

You will need to use your instincts about this one; given the taut nerves and hurt feelings in stereotyping and scapegoating, such conversations are not always possible. But when you feel they are, initiate them. Go ahead and apologize to the person next to you whom you momentarily offended with your preemptive scrutiny, tell her you realize why you behaved badly, and see where the conversation leads. If you are on the receiving end of the bad

behavior, call the person on it and let him know —
whether tactfully or not — that he ought to reflect more
on his actions. As I say, sometimes this just can't be managed, and you need to take your anger or your shame and
move on. But sometimes it can. And if we, the actual passengers and pedestrians dealing personally with the repercussions of the "War on Terror," won't take on these
issues, who will?

2

Traveling in Terror: Self-Protection versus Excess Baggage

T raveling in America isn't what it used to be — especially flying. Gone are the days when we waltzed through a brief metal scan with a smile at the guards, and when we could stroll through security without a ticket to meet arriving friends or loved ones at their gate.

Today at major airports we wait in block-long lines to be ID'd, show our tickets, have our luggage scanned, remove half our clothes and our shoes, and be quizzed or have our carry-ons opened and searched on the spot if anything looks funny. And if our number comes up — or if we fit certain profiles — we are relegated to the dreaded "full search" line, whence, if things go badly, we could find ourselves "asked" to step into a back room for questioning.

Fear, and official alert, have receded from the fever pitch of the months immediately following September 11, 2001, although they could easily spike once again in the event of another attack. But suspicion remains part of the personal routine. Signs and warnings remind us to watch for hints of terrorism, as if we have the power to clearly discern the signals. An official placard posted in the Washington, D.C., subway, for example, exhorted riders to be on the lookout for the following markers of possible terrorist intent:

- Someone acting nervous or sweating, carrying a sprayer bottle or aerosol canister, or wearing inappropriate clothes such as an unusually baggy jacket.
- Unattended bags, packages, boxes, backpacks, etc.
- Smoke or odd smells.

Okay, an aerosol canister is pretty odd. And unattended packages, sure, if you can ascertain within your few stops that they have been abandoned. But a baggy jacket? Smoke or odd smells? Sweating? Any of these could indict a sizable proportion of the subway riders of any major metropolis.

In the name of security, somebody is playing fast and loose with our powers of vigilance. And we travelers know it. We know that the "don't fear it, fight it" mantra regarding terrorism works much better in an ad campaign than in the real life of a passenger. As I write, the lawsuits filed by people wrongly detained and removed from planes are accumulating. The awkward glances and hurt feelings between passengers are legion. And the frustration and agitation of those on both sides of this impossible set of distinctions are palpable.

So what are we passengers supposed to do to feel safe? And if we fall within the suspect profiles, how are we supposed to feel and react?

There is, as we all know, no such thing as absolute safety. Things happen, and some of them we cannot personally prevent. But the real questions for all of us about terrorism are, What can you and I *reasonably* expect to be able to do to protect ourselves? and Where is the line between acceptable caution and unacceptable (and antisocial) suspicion?

We have all heard the boilerplate statistics about our being safer aboard a plane than we are driving to the airport. They are true, but they do not do much to soothe our fears about flying because they do not address what we can or cannot *do* to be safer.

To gain some clarity about the actual terrorism risks we are exposed to and whether they are within or beyond our personal control, let's look at some facts:

- As I write, most of the checked baggage and cargo on a typical flight out of an American airport is not inspected by airline or Transportation Security Authority (TSA) personnel. Electronic screening is performed, although with questionable effectiveness given the limitations of the technology and the inadequacies of TSA funding. And although random spot checks of baggage are used as a deterrent to terrorists, the fact is that most baggage and nearly all cargo do not receive individual human attention, no matter how carefully passengers themselves are inspected or searched.

- As of now, American long-distance trains and buses perform no routine security screening of checked or carry-on baggage whatsoever.
- As of this writing, only 5 percent of the containers arriving in American ports from overseas are inspected or screened for explosives, toxins, or other means of destruction. Ninety-five percent are unloaded from ships and go directly inland — to stores, businesses, and government — with no scrutiny whatsoever of their contents.

What this means for you and me is the following: We leave our houses (stocked with purchased items that came out of uninspected freight containers), drive toward the airport (at greater risk of death than on our upcoming flight), weave in and out among dozens of trucks carrying even more freight from unscrutinized containers, pull up at an airport where no cars are screened for explosives, and board a plane on which most of the checked baggage and cargo has not been inspected by personnel.

So how is it, exactly, that we are effectively protecting ourselves from risk by then leveling our gaze at a passenger of a particular skin color or cultural costuming?

Enter the fallback rationalization for casual profiling: that a passenger's apparent ethnicity or nationality may be a marker for increased risk of their having terrorist intent — say, having checked a bag with a bomb in it, or planning to break into the cockpit. But again, this excuse disintegrates upon contact with logic. Despite warnings in airports, it is relatively easy to swap or tamper with an inattentive stranger's bags in a busy airport. As anti-American fervor spreads globally, it is also more and more feasible — despite the ethnocentric protests of the Ann Coulters of the world — for non-Arabic-looking recruits to carry out terrorist plots.

But the definitive argument against passenger-on-passenger profiling is this: For any rare passenger of Arabic background who might actually merit suspicion on any given day, there are literally millions of ordinary, innocent travelers of Arabic descent who deserve and desire to be treated exactly like everyone else — with no sidelong glances, no muttered or joking comments, and no politely veiled ethnically motivated requests from airline agents to step out of line and answer a few questions.

Why, after all, in this age of bank-vault cockpit doors, should legions of blameless passengers bear the brunt of fear, through the ugliness of profiling, about the shortcomings of a system that has failed up front to fully monitor the greater threat of onboard baggage, not to mention the stunningly unaddressed terrorism risks of incoming foreign freight?

Still not convinced? Listen to security consultant Gavin de Becker, author of *The Gift of Fear* and *Fear Less*, books about protecting oneself from violent crime and post-9/11 terrorism, respectively: "I believe with substantial certainty that the hijacking of commercial jets the way it's been done in the past is just that: a thing of the past. *It is over.* [Emphasis his.] For forty years hijackers gained the cooperation and compliance of passengers through the promise of safety or the threat of harm. Neither of those promises will work anymore."[1]

It makes sense. If you were a terrorist, would you repeat a method that has now spurred the greatest preventive response in the history of American transportation? And that has galvanized passengers to the point of excess watchfulness? A mere look at past experience makes it clear that terrorists at this level of sophistication are always seeking the next unexpected method, the next surprise tactic. The smart money is not in sweating over the man seated next to us on a plane, but in scanning our society for terrorism opportunities as yet unexploited. Sadly, there are plenty, and they are the ones that deserve more of our attention.

Why don't they get the attention they deserve? Because the idea of "safety from terrorism" has been politicized. Truly effective terrorism prevention is both difficult and costly for government and undesirably expensive for private companies such as shippers. As a result, those charged with our safety have sought an antiterrorism enterprise they can get their hands around within the limits of the resources and political will at hand. Their solution, so far, has been to erect a massive, high-profile system for personally screening passengers as we board planes — a system of questionable effectiveness but undeniably high political visibility. Journalistic and NGO reports continue to reveal the sometimes alarming holes in airport security,[2] and the rules for dangerous carry-on items change for seemingly spurious reasons (matches were forbidden, now they are allowed; small scissors were a risk, now they are okay). But the huge spectacle of passenger screening, and the inconvenience it causes for you and me when we fly, at least creates the impression that something is being done.

All of which means that, in the absence of broader and deeper security measures that would address the areas of greatest risk, the spotlight has instead been placed on passenger screening and passenger vigilance. That is, the authorities watch the passengers, and we passengers watch one another.

And this brings us back to the basic question: What can you and I actually do, walking through that terminal or aboard that train or bus or plane, that might realistically make a difference? And at what point are we as passengers chasing our tails — and abusing people's civil rights and feelings — for the mere sake of symbolic action that bears no relation to our safety?

I make no pretense of detailed expertise in the how-tos of emergency or urgently dangerous situations. For that, I refer you to the writings of de Becker and others who specialize in safety. But in general, what appears sensible from the evidence we have so far is that you follow the common-sense rules posted and repeated over the PA systems in air, train, and bus terminals: Keep your hands and your eyes on your luggage, do not accept carry-on gifts from strangers, and notify authorities if you see anything defensibly suspicious (a swarthy man with a scowl on his face does not qualify; a man handing another a knife does).

Beyond that, I suggest these considerations for sanely prudent behavior in the company of other passengers.

Survival Suggestions

1. Understand that your sense of danger has been skewed.

For political reasons, the personal passenger screening and scrutiny channels of American transportation security have been emphasized above critically neglected channels such as port and baggage inspection. You need to know that while flying (or riding a train or a bus) remains remarkably safe in comparison to other things you routinely do, stereotyped cues of danger posed by other passengers have been hyped in relation to the other, broader risks. Understand that your suspicion of a brown-skinned man or woman in a colorful, flowing costume — absent any tangibly suspicious behavior — is nothing but ill-informed, antisocial behavior. It will not make you safer. It will only make you uglier.

2. Let behavior be your guide for scrutinizing others.

Judge people by what they do, not by their apparent ethnicity or culture. A person appearing to hide a heavy object beneath his or her clothing is one thing. A person simply appearing to be Middle Eastern and in a bad mood is quite another. For a sense of how to physically read true threats posed by others, I recommend Gavin de Becker's previously mentioned books *The Gift of Fear* and *Fear Less*,[3] in which he explains cues that he calls "pre-incident indicators" — physical signals of a person's intent to do harm. De Becker places a high value on honoring one's intuition — a chancy enterprise, in my view, in an era in which certain excessive suspicions have become reflexive — but he has much of value to say in both books about how people behave under stress and how the media distort our sense of risk.

3. If you behave unfairly toward someone, own it.

If you behave badly, and you know it — treating a person with suspicion, for example, who in fact demonstrates complete innocence, or making a terrorism-related ethnic remark that is overheard by a passenger of that group — do not cringe in the belief that you are powerless to remedy (or at least atone for) your misbehavior. Step up and own what you have done. This is, of course, a judgment call on your part; an infuriated person may be best left alone. There are times when you need to cut your losses and slink away. But if you see an opportunity to apologize, do so. Let the person know that you see your mistake, and you regret it. It's the very least you can do. Perhaps he will accept your apology. Perhaps he will not. But maybe your willingness to engage him in the moment will open up a meaningful, if brief, exchange. After all, if you are not willing to confront stereotype on this basic and personal a level, when will you be?

4. If you feel unfairly scrutinized by another passenger, let him or her know.

If you find yourself the object of unwarranted suspicion by another passenger, it is your decision, and yours alone, how to react. It is not your job to educate all bigoted or ill-informed people, nor is it your responsibility to interrupt your attempt at a peaceful flight in order to upbraid a jerk. You have the right to define how and when you choose to respond. At those times when you elect to do so, it may relieve you of some anger as well as provide a much-needed lesson to someone who clearly needs to think more about the meaning of their actions. Of course, if you are profiled or otherwise mistreated by airline or security personnel, things escalate to an a entirely different level. Legal matters can come into play, with serious repercussions for both you and the airline. The judgment about how best to take care of yourself is again yours to make. Know, however, that an airline, or any other carrier, that suffers consequences for unfair treatment of passengers will be less likely to repeat it.

3

Still Caught in Katrina: Facing Our Ongoing Storm of Race and Class

elcome to another country:
W On a sodden embankment, a bloated corpse rots in the hot sun for days while passersby remain preoccupied with their own desperation to survive.

On a sun-baked, filth-strewn superhighway, crowds of parched, partially clothed residents are held at gunpoint by panicky police officers in virtual open stockades.

On a street in plain public view, a man lies groaning in agony for want of life-sustaining medication. He eventually dies on the pavement.

Within the rank twilight of a darkened stadium dome with no electricity or running water or sewage facilities, clumps of traumatized men, women, and children huddle to try to sleep and protect themselves. They urinate and defecate on the ground in whatever semblance of privacy they can find. The dome's upper floors harbor even worse dangers. The entire place reeks with the overwhelming stench of unwashed bodies, sickness, and human waste. Outside, most of those who try to escape are blocked by armed police.

In the nation's capital, despite the fact that top officials have been accurately advised of the catastrophic potential of the coming hurricane, the actions needed to deliver needed federal help in time to avert disaster do not happen.

Meanwhile, on television, a reporter shocked to the point of outrage stands amid the surreal carnage and repeats again and again to the camera that in spite of promised government action, "Nothing is happening! Nothing is happening!"

Welcome to another country: the one within American borders that so many of us never see, think about, or visit.

Hurricane Katrina did not create the "other America." It just blew the roof off of it so that our entire nation was forced to face it.

For as long as there has been an America, in fact, there have been "other Americas": the nations of the original inhabitants of this land; the cultures and communities of slaves imported for forced labor from the African continent, and, after Emancipation, their descendants; the lives and experiences of diverse peoples of Hispanic descent; of Jewish descent, and of Irish descent, to take a few examples.

What the Hurricane Katrina episode did in August and September of 2005, however, was to dramatically display to the world a particular "other America" whose meaning had been so long ignored as to render it invisible to the American mainstream — except as a place to avoid. When these decades of smug neglect and disenfranchisement culminated in globally televised human suffering on a biblical scale in the poorest, blackest sections of the city of New Orleans, the shock to the national psyche was akin to a hammer blow to the solar plexus.

How could this happen in America? asked Democrats, Republicans, liberals, and conservatives alike as images and stories of grotesquely preventable tragedies cascaded across television screens nationwide: dead babies, people drowned in their attics, ballooned corpses floating serenely down main streets, hysterical survivors screaming for lost family members, residents waving for help while trapped for days on the roofs of houses, the masses of the sick and the hungry hemmed in at gunpoint by terrified cops for whom official protocol had dissolved in the face of a universal desperation to simply get out alive.

And therein lay the hard truth that slashed open the national conscience during the Katrina media spectacle: what looked like scenes from some distant, poorly governed nation depicted, in fact, a major city in the United States of America.

The Katrina debacle gave the American mainstream a brutally unavoidable window on the nation's astounding neglect of the black urban poor. It did so precisely because the expected response of American government, and the subsequent spectacular failure of government to meet this expectation, were so starkly and dramatically laid bare by the facts on the ground. Here was one case in which white suburbanites did not have to take black leaders' word for it that impoverished black people were being recklessly mistreated. It was right there on national television for all to see.

The Katrina tragedy and its agonizing aftermath were and are, of course, awash in both race and economic class. Those marooned in New Orleans — aside from the relative few who had the means to leave but simply stayed — were stuck there because they did not have cars, they lacked money, and they had nowhere to go. They were overwhelmingly black and poor. They were the people who — in the electoral calculus of a presidential administration that focused its appeal on the far right and the white middle class — did not count, both in terms of votes and in terms of policy. To be sure, the Bush agenda's specific abuse of poor blacks, via vote-counting shenanigans and the militarized policing and draconian sentencing mandates of the War on Drugs, took for granted the venerable assumption that the black poor can be mistreated without widespread popular outcry. But it also involved a broader sort of exclusionism that ignored the interests of a group, any group, in direct proportion to that group's lack of power.

The poorest of the black inner-city poor, tagged for years as an "underclass" scurrying somewhere beneath America's basement, perfectly filled the bill as a politically powerless constituency to be deliberately disregarded while the administration went ahead with its political business. Even more politically useful was the ease with which the poor black underclass could be popularly demonized by persuasive media personalities as predators, druggies, and layabouts, providing a powerful distraction for the white middle and working classes while the administration proceeded with its own narrow domestic and foreign priorities.

All of which means that, to the Washington administration in power at the time, ignoring the looming catastrophe among trapped poor blacks while Katrina bore down on New Orleans was a downright reflexive reaction. The essential facts of this stupendous blowing off of the invisible denizens of low-income New Orleans have been established beyond dispute, and we do not need to catalogue them in detail here. But a quick review of what happened explains the heat of the ensuing outrage, and shows us why Katrina became the flash point for the national moral scandal of the "two Americas."

- In 2003 President Bush appointed Michael D. Brown, a Bush campaign supporter with no disaster management experience — in his last position he worked for the International Arabian Horse Association — to head the Federal Emergency Management Agency (FEMA), which oversees response to major disasters. In the following months, reports emerged of sinking morale and shrinking competency in the agency as career disaster professionals were replaced or marginalized by political appointees who favored cutting the agency's budgets and its mission. FEMA was also folded into the recently created Department of Homeland Security, a move that boded ill for FEMA's preparation to deal with national disasters, its long-designated focus.
- As Katrina approached New Orleans in late August 2005, weather experts predicted a "storm of the century" with apocalyptic potential for those in its path. The White House was advised of this days before the storm hit. Bush was on vacation,

but reportedly was told. The White House neither took nor ordered any special action; Bush explained afterward that he left the job to Brown and FEMA. An aggravating fact is that the Bush administration had earlier cut funding to the state of Louisiana for the strengthening of levees against flooding.

- Meanwhile, when the storm smashed into New Orleans on August 29, both city and state governments were immediately and completely overwhelmed. Ray Nagin, the city's business-friendly mayor, lost precious time waiting for business approval of critical emergency plans, and in any case neither he nor the state's governor, Kathleen Blanco, had anywhere near the resources at their disposal to manage the disaster.

- FEMA director Brown, for his part, ordered no large-scale federal mobilization when the storm hit or for days afterward, during which the city's hopeless situation was constantly displayed in the media. Brown's defense after he came under fire was that he had been waiting to be "asked" for help, to which Mayor Nagin replied with a furious, obscenity-laden radio tirade that made national news.[1]

- On the night of August 29, Brown (according to his later account)[2] told the White House that a levee above New Orleans had broken, which exponentially worsened the flooding and casualties. Brown's account of this rebutted White House claims that it didn't learn of the levee break until later.

- As media and voter outrage swelled at the news from New Orleans, President Bush eventually left his ranch vacation and made a trip to the city, where he was criticized for his lighthearted manner (he joked, for example, about the times he had partied in nearby Houston). He returned several more times to New Orleans with sober-faced promises of federal aid. As of this writing, a year after the hurricane, less than half of the more than $100 billion in federally allocated aid had been spent, and recovery was mired in red tape, waste, and fraud.[3]
- Further feeding popular outrage was a television interview with Homeland Security chief Michael Chertoff, in which he displayed, to the reporter's (and many viewers') amazement, utter ignorance of the abject suffering that reporters were witnessing in the city.
- Reporters began to speak openly about what was obvious in the television and print images from New Orleans: Nearly all of the residents trapped in the city's flood, from which many others had escaped, were poor and black.
- Another racial issue that emerged was controversy over major media referring to these overwhelmingly black evacuees as "refugees," as if they were arrivals from the other side of the world who now begged Americans for help rather than being full American citizens themselves. This contrasted with what reporters had tended to call the mostly white casualties of 9/11: victims, evacuees, survivors, heroes. This distinction tended to reflect the mainstream attitude of the alienness of poor, black, ghettoized

citizens. Similarly, media descriptions of blacks as "looting" deserted stores and whites as "finding" supplies in such stores highlighted racial stereotypes and further inflamed resentments.[4]

- Residents, pundits, and Republican and Democratic politicians piled on to savage FEMA chief Brown, who resigned in disgrace, and Bush, who admitted an inadequacy of response but was slow to take personal responsibility. A full year after the disaster, a *New York Times/CBS News* poll showed that 51 percent of Americans disapproved of Bush's response to Katrina.[5]

- As of this writing, there were more than 1,800 confirmed deaths from Katrina — of which more than 1,500 were in Louisiana — and hundreds more unaccounted for.[6] The total number of deaths may never be known. At least 200,000 evacuees had still not returned.[7] Only 17 percent of the New Orleans city buses were in use, half the routes were open, and gas and electricity service were at 40 and 60 percent of pre-Katrina levels respectively.[8] Estimated damage from the storm was at least $80 billion,[9] and the city of New Orleans was hundreds of millions of dollars in debt.[10]

Is it any wonder, then, that the Katrina story has become a parable for our nation's lingering separate and unequal treatment of citizens? To see the curtain pulled back on the national stage to reveal the long-term realities of de facto apartheid was dramatic enough. But to also see the glaring double standard in how our government viewed the safety of a poor black community in comparison with, say, that of a comfortable white middle-class community was devastating. It was a moment of unintentional honesty in which our government's behavior bespoke a long-denied truth: *We simply do not care very much about poor black communities, and it is our ingrained habit to not pay as much attention to them as we do to others.*

This is the chord that Katrina struck. This is the point of divergence between the mainstream American point of view, in which neighborhoods afflicted with drug wars and bombed-out houses and scarce jobs and war-zone schools are feared but largely out of sight except for crime news, and the vantage point of those who live in these neighborhoods or who empathize with them. In this clash of worlds, Katrina blew down the wall between them. Even more potently, Katrina put directly in all Americans' faces the foul reality that our society does not treat its citizens equally on as basic a moral matter as the essential human right to receive all possible help in a natural disaster.

In that sense, the Katrina response and its aftermath is an unnatural disaster, manufactured by bigotry and human unfairness. And this is a realization that sticks deeply in the craw of a nation that calls itself a democracy.

We have choices as to what to do with this information. We can use the jagged opening afforded by the Katrina disaster, with all its continuing tragedy and needless injustice, as a portal through which to push more of our attention and resources to places where they are sorely needed: communities where local jobs are either virtually nonexistent or an economic joke that offers nothing like a living wage or realistic benefits; where despair leads to drug use, and drug use ravages families and sends children to the streets to die from drugs or from drug-driven bullets; where drug addicts wait so long for admission to underfunded rehab facilities that they can't hold out any longer and succumb to addiction; where crumbling schools teach kids that they cannot learn; where being treated with fear and contempt by the larger society teaches kids to lash out like kamikaze avengers.

Or we can close the portal once more, retreat into mistrust and cynicism, lock our minds and our car doors, and surrender to the rules of "otherness" that hold us, we think, safely apart.

How long, after all, can we continue to go about our everyday lives as citizens and taxpayers — the legal owners and underwriters of these American injustices — without at some point feeling overcome by outrage and shame at what is done (and not done) in our name and with our money?

Only until the next storm comes along.

Survival Suggestions

1. Find a way to make a difference.

Don't just shake your head at the unfairness on the streets and on the television news. Make a decision that you are going to be part of a force for change. It might be supporting a group pushing for more funding for public schools. It might be running for public office on a platform of serving the interests of the public instead of those of private campaign contributors. It might be joining a series of demonstrations demanding adequate funding for drug treatment. It might be pushing local or state leaders to approve a living wage law. It might be volunteering as a tutor or a mentor to help one person, or five, gain a grasp on the world. Decide what you can do. Then do it.

2. Vote your beliefs.

Bring your social principles to the voting booth. Let candidates know that you will not support them unless they support the policies you value most highly. We have "two Americas" because our leaders feel they have our permission to maintain two Americas: through counterproductive drug laws, lack of support for massive job training and school funding, and policies favoring private development over public services and programs. Let politicians know that if they don't get with the program, you will vote them out. The hard Right has been doing this for years. It is time for fairer-minded Americans to consciously use our leverage.

3. Don't fool yourself. Respect differences in experience.

Embracing the truths exposed by Katrina is no excuse to waltz into a community you know nothing about and declare yourself available as a community improver. Nor is it an excuse for you to lambaste well-meaning middle-class people about their personal responsibility for a poor community's suffering. No real work will get done unless those on all sides respect, for starters, how their experiences differ. A certain amount of translation and (quite literally) orientation to one another's worlds is needed. My best suggestion is that you find an organization that is already doing this kind of work — and that knows how it should be done — and become a part of it.

4

Survival and Stereotype on the Street

A white couple is walking after dark on a city sidewalk. Approaching them are two young black males, side by side in their baggy jeans and loose jackets. They could be high school seniors with B-minus averages and new haircuts, walking to a girlfriend's birthday party. They could be high school dropouts, minnows in the street-drug food chain who carry cheap guns because their rivals carry cheap guns. They could be two cousins who work the late shift together at McDonald's. The approaching white couple does not know who these young men are, but they feel afraid: the baggy clothes, the big shoes, the swaying walk. Danger. The whites wonder: Cross the street? Turn around?

No *other pedestrians nearby. The two young black men watch them and sneer. They laugh inside at the scare film playing behind the white couple's frozen stare. Twenty feet. Ten feet. Cold eyes meet cold eyes.*

Cut to broad daylight. An elevator door opens, and a black man (he sells office supplies) comes face-to-face with a white female stranger (she sells insurance). Instantly, as if cued, she tightens her hold on her purse, locking her elbow inward for a better grip. She doesn't think about it. She just does it. She has never had her purse snatched. She does, however, watch a lot of local TV news and talk to her friends, and from what she has seen and heard a lot of street crime seems to involve black men. Seven months from now she will be robbed — accosted from behind by a white man she never saw coming. But right now, all she knows is that she is within reach of a black man. And she keeps a fierce grip on that purse.

Cut to a street corner. A white man (he keeps a company's books) quickly reaches to pat his own wallet pocket just as a black man (he is a well-known area musician) starts to pass him on the street. The gesture is subtle. Reflexive. Unmistakable. It is a motion the white bookkeeper makes several times a day in public, and it is one the black musician sees many times a day. The moment passes. The black musician refrains, as always, from attempting to pick the white man's pocket. The bodies diverge: an honest white citizen, ever on guard, and an honest black citizen, treated, for one long instant, as a felon. They will never meet again.

Cut to a poor white neighborhood at dusk. The inhabitants are what an elderly black lady in gold jewelry would lower her voice to call "poor white trash." A black man is traveling here on foot. He did not plan to walk this way. But here he is. Four young white men in tank tops and T-shirts stand on a stoop. They stop their conversation to look at the black man. They could be lifelong neighbors occupied with their own business. They could be hip-hop fans who wish they were as cool as they perceive black men to be. They could be jobless and already drunk and eager to kick some goddamned nigger's ass. They could be cautious, sensing the black man sensing them. The black man doesn't know who they are, but he fears he recognizes them: faces from Bensonhurst and South Boston and every other white urban village from which an errant black man has failed to return. And now they are watching him watch them, and all are silent.

What a way to travel. Too often, our worst habits and fantasies masquerade as intuition; we strain our eyes watching for color and in the process lose all our other senses. But at other times our fearful reactions serve us well, and we know it. This is a dangerous world, and some parts of it are more dangerous than others.

With the crime and the rage and the risks out there, the stakes seem too high for us to exercise anything but caution — to grip our purses, check for our wallets, prepare for escape. Do we bruise sensibilities? Make bigoted presumptions? *Well,* we say, *too bad.* Nor is this a simple matter of nonblacks stereotyping blacks and vice-versa. Some especially potent racially coded fears are embraced by nonblacks and blacks alike, particularly along class lines. As one middle-class black woman declared to me about her automatic avoidance of young black males on the street at night: "Hey, sorry, but I'm making it home *alive.*"

The images are at their most fearsome, though, when we stray into an ethnically unfamiliar neighborhood. America's brutal racial history has taught us all well. In many a community, any ethnic "trespasser" is fiercely alert for even the slightest scent of blood on the wind. Today's noxious climate of crime, rage, and general dread has further poisoned our air.

These are not good economic times for most Americans, whether poor or middle-class. With an economy drained by war, tax cuts slanted toward the rich, fleeing jobs, and a business-friendly regulatory climate, many whites have seen their standards of living plummet and their savings evaporate, and are embittered about the distribution of what is left of the country's resources. Many blacks have seen inner-city communities decline from poverty into outright apocalypse while their own government imprisons more and more black men and cuts efforts against poverty, joblessness, and discrimination. They feel betrayed as never before.

The fiery search for blame, stoked in recent years by Rage Talk media, is blistering: it's the lazy blacks; it's single mothers; it's white racists bent upon annihilating African Americans as a people; it's greedy Jews; it's greedy Asian storekeepers; it's Arabs who want to destroy Western life; it's swarming illegal immigrants; it's gays out to ruin what's left of the family; it's godlessness; it's affirmative action; it's government.

What makes it hard, on the street, for so many of us to reconcile our sense of fairness with our sense of fear is that there *are* dangers, and there *are* reasons to be afraid in certain places and under certain circumstances. Only a fool or a well-meaning naïf in denial of these perils would ignore them. Poverty nurtures property crime because people who cannot afford things they need or want have an incentive to steal them. Poverty also nurtures violent nonproperty crime — domestic violence, arguments that turn deadly — because of accumulated rage and a sense of powerlessness. And poverty nurtures addictive drug use as an escape as well, with all of its attendant ills: family disarray, health deterioration, the spread of AIDS, burglaries and robberies to feed drug habits, and shootings between drug-trade rivals (often claiming bystanders as well as the intended targets).

And so impoverished, drug-riddled neighborhoods, and sometimes the neighborhoods bordering them, are indeed often more dangerous places to live or pass through than economically healthier neighborhoods or suburbs, where illegal drug use takes place within comfortable living rooms and most residents feel neither the daily economic panic nor the anger that permeates life in our poorest communities.

In cities where most of the poorest people are black, and where most of the violent crime is therefore in black communities (claiming mostly black victims, by the way), and where public schools and social services are chronically underfunded and understaffed due to an inadequate tax base, black youth do, not surprisingly, commit crimes at a rate greater than their proportion in the population. In Baltimore, where I live, there are 200 to 300 homicides a year, mostly drug-related, one out of every five young black men is in jail, and more than half of the city's young black males are either incarcerated or under the supervision of the criminal justice system.[1] These are heartbreaking statistics, and they indict our entire society. They also mean, however, that a pedestrian's refusing to view a young black man suspiciously in order to avoid being a "racist" is naive and pointless. The fact is that too many of our young black men have become dangers to themselves and others. Ignoring them, or refusing to scrutinize them with ordinary care, helps no one.

But it's a two-way street. There are areas where blacks traveling alone or in groups have reason to feel threatened. If he were alive, you could ask James Byrd, the black man dragged by whites behind a pickup truck in Texas until his body was torn apart, about this. There are, as well, places where gay Americans do not feel safe; if he were still living, Matthew Shepard, the young gay man beaten and left to die in rural Wyoming, could fill you in on the details. Arab Americans, in the wake of the rise in hate crimes since 9/11, also have ample proof of the risks that they face in their routine travels.

So what is the answer for those of us who want to be safe without stereotyping?

Sadly, there is no solution that will assure you of both absolute safety and complete freedom from wrongly judging others. It ain't gonna happen. Judging danger is an art, not a science, and in a society as dangerous as ours, imprecision and error are guaranteed. You will make mistakes.

You will also, however, have the obligation to read cues and dangers in as well-informed a manner as possible. And the way to do that is to free your instincts from the harmful influence of messages that distort your sense of danger and vulnerability, especially in the presence of young black men. Whether you know it or not, you are surrounded by such hyped-up messages, largely from mass media, and if you are not careful you will be prone to accept their impact as instinct when in fact it is the opposite:

amplified fear. Local TV news stations, in particular, tend to boost their viewership ratings and their profits by weighting their coverage with murders, car crashes, and other dramatic telegenic events. Viewers, bathed daily in this artificially concentrated stream of violence and danger, come away with a profoundly warped sense of their own risk of violent harm. But they don't know it.

Instead of succumbing to cultural stereotyping and false clues, you need to rescue your basic instincts for perceiving threats and learn how to trust your ability to observe *what is happening around you right now.* Forget the week's twenty crime stories on the television news or your friend's tale of having been robbed or your having heard "nigger" yelled at you from a jacked-up Trans Am in some white neighborhood. You do not live in a scripted scene from TV or in your past. You live among people who are who they are, not who you preconceive them to be. If you have good reason, from your own specifically local experience or from concrete local advice, to avoid certain places or to exercise care, then do so, especially at night. Do the don't-fuck-with-me walk. Keep your car doors locked no matter where you are (you should; it's safer in the event of an accident). Do not display valuables. Be alert. But admit that there is much about the people around you that you simply do not know. And most of the time, preemptive paranoia will only blind you.

You need to know that within all of us is a prerecorded sound track of canned racial beliefs, like personal elevator music, rendering us deaf to the actual world. Like figures in B movies or slasher films, we become possessed by scripts — "that black man might try for my purse," "that white woman is going to cringe away from me" —

to the point where we can drown out our own ability to perceive what is actually going on. We never reach the stage of comparing actual events with our preconceptions because we never get *past* our preconceptions.

But again, here is the hard part: *these preconceptions are neither wholly truth nor wholly lies.* White pedestrians *have* been attacked by groups of vengeful black youths. A black man *was* dragged behind a pickup truck in Texas until his head and an arm came off. White commuters *have* been shot execution-style on trains. Black teenagers *have* been chased and murdered by mobs in depressed white communities. At the same time, it is possible for me as a black man to go fly-fishing in the open country of the West or make my casual way through any number of unfamiliar white neighborhoods on the strength of my awareness of potential dangers, without the paralyzing presumption that I will be harmed. Black men do it every day without ending up on the evening news. And it is just as feasible and common for whites to travel through most black neighborhoods without having to run for their lives.

The self-protective antidote to prefabricated racial hysteria, then, is for all of us to come to our senses, to re-claim common sense from implanted panic and fury. In the end, our only real personal protection — our best hope for preserving our humanity, as well as our skins, whether on a back road or a packed city street — lies in our ability to see, hear, think, and act clearly. There will indeed be threats against which we need to protect ourselves, whether through caution or combat. But locking ourselves into a stance of rigid defensiveness will not help. Like a boxer who stays behind his gloves, terrified of giving his opponent an opening, we await and assure our own defeat.

So what should you do on the street? Pay attention. Are people eyeing you or ignoring you? Is that really a hostile group of characters hovering in your vicinity, or are you *interpreting* a black teenager in a big jacket, or a group of white men in T-shirts leaning against a car, as hostile? What kinds of expressions do you read on people's faces? How do they act as you approach them? After you have passed them?

There are of course blocks and whole neighborhoods where, whether due to racial tension or a high crime rate in general, you simply don't want to be, at least not alone. There are many, many more areas where anyone can walk unmolested, and perhaps even unnoticed. Exercise the usual care; brightly lit or crowded places are obviously safer than isolated or darkened ones. Learn about your surroundings in advance. Fear and vulnerability are like loud clothing: they make you an obvious mark. A rule of thumb is that if you are not able to move with a reasonable amount of self-assurance in a given setting, you don't belong there. You yourself can judge what a "reasonable amount" is. Whatever you do, base your actions on what is actually happening, and nothing more. Or you may attract precisely the attention that you most fear.

If you are white, here is a little tip: Black Americans are far more accustomed to being around you than you are to being around them. Sheer numbers force nearly all African Americans to interact regularly with whites, while, as you probably know, there are many whites who spend little or no significant time around black people. Many black people therefore know you better than you know them. Your presence in their lives or in their neighborhoods is not as worthy of notice as you might think. Don't flatter yourself into believing that you're a bigger attraction than you are. Be prepared to react, as you would in any situation, when the vibe is bad and you have the sense of being a target. But treat any black neighborhood as what it is: a community, with a variety of people and attitudes. Just like a white neighborhood.

If you are black and trying your best to keep paranoia in check, you would do well to remember that time-worn moral: Don't do them the way that they do us. You have learned, justifiably, to have a hair-trigger reaction when it comes to white racism, and to expect flagrant and sometimes violent bigotry from some whites. The redneck stereotype of poor whites is a potent one among many blacks, as are countless other generalizations and suspicions. But think about how crazy it makes you to hear white suburbanites prattle on about "those people" — by which they mean you, your friends, and your family. Do you really want to adopt such a system of belief? Are you really so fragile that you need to sheathe yourself in a preemptive dislike of whites, huddling in constant fear of rejection or anger? As black people, we can protect ourselves perfectly well from bodily and psychological attack without needing to skulk through life, claws extended and hair standing on end.

Once, in San Francisco, as my cousin and I were standing at a crosswalk, a white woman in the nearest car looked at us nervously, then conspicuously leaned over and locked her door. I flinched, as if stung, and made a sarcastic remark to my cousin, who glanced at me and in his typically laconic way said, "Who cares? She's worried. I'm not." Then he changed the subject. I stared at him, dumbfounded by his offhand denial of what I felt certain must have gnawed at his gut the way it gnawed at mine. But then it began to register: he really didn't care. I was the one incapacitated by some stranger's display of fear. I had in fact looked at her, which is why I noticed her reaction to us in the first place. I remember having said to myself, "I'll bet she locks her car door." And, as if to fulfill my prophesy, she did. Was it my fault that she was afraid? No. Was it because I was male? Was it because I was black and male? Likely.

But whatever the case, my preoccupation with her perception of me — my need to see how she saw me — was a surrender of self. What if instead I been too busy talking with my cousin, too busy being who I am, to have been affected by someone's peripheral paranoia? I would have served myself instead of her. Black men need to know how to do this. Allowing the momentary hijacking of our sense of self by random acts of fear or hate — call it guerrilla racism — is bad for us. Literally. The high rates of hypertension, stroke, and heart disease among African-American males bear brutal witness to the problem. Do not volunteer yourself as a casualty. Let those with the illness, those who caricature and misrepresent you, be the ones consumed.

My older sister recalls a conversation she once had with an elderly black woman about handling personal incidents of racism. The older woman told her how, some years earlier, she and several black female friends were sightseeing in a southern city when a carful of white youths roared alongside, yelled "Nigger!" and other epithets, and sped off. The woman finished her story by remarking, placidly, that she and her friends had gone on to have a perfectly marvelous afternoon. My sister, astonished at the woman's composure, asked, "But didn't the episode with the white boys completely wreck your day?" The woman gave her a surprised look. "Why should it? It was pure foolishness."

It will serve us well to keep this in mind as we walk the streets.

Survival Suggestions

1. Understand that your sense of endangerment has been hyped.

I suggest that you skip local TV news altogether; its chief news value is for weather and sports. If you must watch it, realize that the amount of depicted violence bears no relation to your actual risks; it is cobbled together as a concentrated mosaic of crime and trauma for the sake of effect, which serves ratings and ad revenues. Do not mistake it for a portrait of actual likelihoods in your daily life.

2. Understand that you do face dangers.

Once you have gained a true baseline of risk, do not be ashamed about being cautious. Be informed. Know where you are going, get local advice about where and where not to be, and respect the fact that socioeconomic realities create dangers. Just as you should not allow broad racial stereotypes to dictate your behavior, you should not deny signs of danger out of an exaggerated fear of appearing "racist."

3. Act according to what people do.

You can fantasize all you like about people's intent. Your best protection is to observe what they do: how they act, how they behave toward you, and what feeling you get from their attention. If it looks bad, cross the street, or find a store or a bar to duck into, or hail a cab out of Dodge. Better yet, determine ahead of time where you'll likely be safe and where you won't.

4. Do more than simply protect yourself.

Protecting your own safety in an unbalanced, angry society is necessary. But it is not enough. What are you doing to address the inequities? What can you offer to increase a kid's chances that he or she will not grow up to pursue a life of preying on others? How can you push for more resources to be shifted toward crime-ridden communities that need jobs and drug treatment centers and decent schools? For a person of conscience, running away from a dangerous young criminal on the street is not sufficient. What will you later do, as a citizen, to help eradicate what creates the dysfunction?

5

Subliminal Training:
Race in Public Transit

R ush hour on board a bus or a train. A blur of bodies, each one moving faster than thought. The flood of oncoming passengers begins to solidify. Our skins jam ever closer with each stop. I sit next to a window, my eyes half closed in the lurching zone between departure and arrival. Dressed conservatively in a tweed jacket and tastefully bold tie, I am an unremarkable man on an unremembered train, as unnoticed as any other commuter. Except for one thing: amid the growing crush, the seat beside me remains empty. At stop after stop, as people come on board, glance around, and seat themselves, a succession of seemingly random individual decisions coalesces into a glaring pattern of unoccupied spaces next to black *males — including me. Soon, the seats beside us are the only ones left. Other passengers remain standing, leaving these seemingly quarantined seats to those desperate souls who board once the car is choked past capacity.*

Though I have seen many white people plunk themselves down without even a glance, I have also seen, over time, a broad pattern of avoidance of black men far too pronounced for measly coincidence. Do you doubt me? Ask any black man. Better yet, begin watching.

This skirt-the-contagion dance is not a purely white-avoiding-black set of moves. I've seen everyone do it: Asians, Hispanics, Jews, other blacks. It can be aimed at Arab Americans as well. And at whites by blacks: On a packed bus in a poor African-American neighborhood, a black teenager makes a grand show of avoiding the seat next to a white woman with red hair. He stops, he glares, he sits elsewhere. The woman is a friend of mine. She is regularly shunned, sneered at, and called names by black strangers when she rides buses. Some black passengers, forced to sit beside her, turn their backs on her entirely, sitting with their feet in the aisle and their bodies hunched away from her in an exaggerated pantomime of revulsion.

And so there you are in your vinyl seat: a white person treated like snow-covered carrion by perfect strangers who have dark skin. And there I am: a personable black man avoided like a jaguar by people who know nothing about me. And there is a law-abiding Arab-American man being treated like a public threat. And the question echoes among us: What in the world are we doing?

The good news is that such behavior — or the black/white element of it, anyway — seems to me to have diminished somewhat in the years since the first edition of *Race Manners* was published. It depends, in part, on where you are: the jammed New York City subway, say, seems to enforce more of a scrambling grab-any-seat ethic than the roomier and less frantic Washington, D.C., Metro, where I see more racial pickiness even today. On buses, and in smaller cities, old patterns can die even harder.

In any case, ethnic-based skirting still happens more often than it should.

In the case of passengers who specifically avoid black males, what they are doing is letting a grim fairy tale wreak havoc with their powers of observation and common sense.

Where does the tale come from? Again, from local television news for a start. From eerily identical news broadcasts, each a grainy video account of poor and uneducated black men netted, like angry Discovery Channel wildebeests, by the police — another in a numbing procession of street crimes. From photographs in the local news section of sullen-looking black youths in handcuffs. From politicians who rail against a scripted cast of enemies to middle-class security: predatory criminals, savage drug addicts, hedonistic single parents who bear free-roaming young. From a dark flood of villains portrayed as disproportionately urban and black. From the shortage of coverage hinting at the larger, less action-packed world in which black children do homework in tenement bedrooms and black parents marry and work long hours — and in which white suburbanites commit felonies within stucco walls.

What Americans get from this single-themed newsreel, along with the pounding paranoid mantra of Rage Talk shows, is a message of fear, reinforced at frequent intervals: Black inner-city people are out of control, and their kids are killers. No wonder, then, that this fear and avoidance of blacks, this tendency to give all African Americans a wide berth, has come to be second nature for so many whites.

Youth brings a nonracial component to the equation. We expect recklessness, a blind lack of restraint, from the young. And with males committing the vast majority of crimes on earth, young males, of all of our potential seatmates on buses and trains, seem most likely to be trouble.

But the young black male is special. He is our darling of perceived deviance, our poster child of ill will and bad blood. For him, we reserve particular apprehension, even in the face of moderating facts. To be sure, black men commit crimes at a rate greater than their proportion of the population (we could debate the social reasons), and in many urban environments this adds a racial element to routine caution on the street. But the fact remains that the vast majority of crimes in the United States, both violent and nonviolent, are committed by white men. Which means that on any given day any American is far more likely to suffer at the hands of a white male criminal than a black criminal. Yet somehow we manage to resist a blanket fear of white males. The double standard is stark and ugly. Many Americans, regardless of race, harbor a fear of African-American males that is wildly, even hysterically, out of proportion with reality.

And sometimes the fear can boil down to an empty seat. I know how it feels to be targeted. I have had so many seats remain empty next to me on jam-packed buses and trains that at a certain point, like many in my position, I have gone numb to the experience. I have learned to override the impulse to be maddened by the daily insult because

I simply can no longer stand to care. I can no longer endure seething through innumerable bus and train rides, striving in vain to make angry eye contact with people for whom avoiding black men has become routine. I can no longer stand the prickles of paranoia, the perception of even coincidental gestures as tiny racial slights, the feeling that my ego is as accessible as public transportation.

When we hear young black urban men speak reverently of "respect," what they mean is that they are starving for the kind of casual, ordinary recognition that whites take for granted. They want what is freely given to most white strangers encountered in public: the benefits of being presumed intelligent, civilized unless shown to be otherwise, presumed decent unless demonstrably repellent. When this most basic of courtesies is consistently denied, the result, among legions of young black men, is an outright obsession with respect that seizes the only power available — aggression — and uses it as a weapon of self-esteem. Can't you see it on the street? The cocky walk, the expansive flinging of arms as if to claim the world, the (corporate-abetted) worship of competitive physical prowess, the idea of a gun, or the threat of one, as hair-trigger personal veto power. "I compel, therefore I am. *Now* try to squelch my existence, bitch." All in pursuit of mere acknowledgment. Such an obsession with everyday acceptance can just as easily grip a black commuter sheathed in a suit and tie — except that, in his case, the violence coils inward. Whether by bus or by train, it makes for a mean, and sometimes brutally short, earthly journey.

As I've suggested with the example of my red-haired friend, racial rejection happens to white people on buses and trains, too. And it hurts. But there is a difference.

Most white people do not shoulder their way through a lifetime of being singled out for hostile caricature. And in the absence of society-wide bashing of the white self-image, they can more easily recover from being snubbed on a bus. Black Americans are not subjected to a media barrage of images of white citizens jacking up helpless yo boys (the dominant media messages, in fact, depict whiteness as a colorless, pleasantly inert state of normalcy). The "home turf" nastiness some black passengers may show a white commuter can best be understood as a sort of revenge. From the standpoint of many blacks, whites have done all but beg to be disliked. To those African Americans inclined to seek easy enemies, embracing a raft of malignant white stereotypes (they are dirty, they are ice-hearted, they have poor home training) can deliver the sweet rush of vindication. Black people who have fallen victim to this influence will seize the opportunity to make ruthlessly public their personal distaste for white people.

Such treatment may come as a shock to some whites. For many black Americans, however, the need for defense against micro-assaults has long since been ingrained into our consciousness. Years of being treated as lepers in close quarters have pushed many blacks, particularly young black males, into razor-wire zones of psychic self-protection — especially in the crowded confines of a bus or train.

And so here you are: a black person or a white person avoided on public transportation. What are you supposed to do?

If you are black and angry, your first move ought to be to take a long step back from all of this ugliness. Look at the situation from a distance. Be aware that you are witnessing, in today's cultic fear of the color of your skin, a form of public insanity. When twenty-third-century historians write of the period in which we now live — in much the same way that historians now view, say, the ordeals of free blacks during the era of legalized slavery in America — they will judge such behavior with sadness and some measure of disbelief.

Take the clinical view for a moment. The whites who avoid sitting next to you know squat about you as a person, and worse, they don't know that they know squat. Like many nonblack Americans who have little experience with black people, they believe the media distortions and the casual intra-white talk about who you are alleged to be. And if they have had even one bad personal experience with an African American, they are prone to embrace the resulting image for life. Psychiatrists tag substituting exaggerated fears for reality as classically delusional. Should you be offended if a diagnosed paranoid schizophrenic refuses to sit beside you on a bus? People who entertain sensational preconceptions of you fall into an analogous category of lunacy, if only for a few moments at a time. Treat them as such. Sit back, read your newspaper or look out of the window, and marvel at a world that regularly offers you extra seating room.

The same clinical approach might work for you if you are an Arab American subjected to such rude and hurtful treatment. The histories are different, to be sure. But the basic principles of fair treatment are the same. On a tactical level, observing craziness for what it is might ease your ride.

Still not satisfied? Want to fight back? You might consider some immediate preemptive moves of your own. For example, place your jacket or satchel on the empty seat next to you, forcing anyone who wants the seat to request it. Sit on the aisle side, effectively blocking the empty window seat until someone asks if they can slide in. Or make it a habit to sit only beside other people. Such gyrations of self-protection, though, strike me as weak and hollow. To what extent, after all, are you really willing to allow other people's behavior to govern your own?

If, on the other hand, you are a black person who singles out white passengers for isolation or abuse, you can now claim the dubious distinction of having assisted in your own dehumanization. Your cooperation in fanning racial ill will among perfect strangers helps to lower black political consciousness to its shallowest possible level — that is, to the same level of blind ethnic belligerence as white supremacism. With your continued assistance, this state of racial barbarism will continue indefinitely.

To many whites, the mere fact of their own seatmate preferences on buses and trains may come as jarring news. How are they supposed to notice patterns so universal as to seem invisible? Freedom from such awareness, after all, comes with being white. American Caucasians can spend their entire lives dancing away from black males or other peoples of color and never even realize it. If you are white, chances are fairly good that you have already done so. Nobody would call you a bad person for doing things of which you are unaware. But if you don't *want* to know, that's another story. So now you've been told. When you take public transit, pay attention. What you see may surprise you.

When and if you find yourself disinclined to sit beside a black male on a bus or train, ask yourself this: If he were white (with the identical manner, clothing, expression, etc.), would you sit down beside him without hesitating? If your answer is no, then avoid him guilt-free. But if the answer is yes, you have a problem. There are plenty of perfectly good reasons for not wanting to sit beside someone: ripe body odor, a rancorous, twisted smile, a beeping package in his hands, an open bottle, the demeanor of a just-opened vein. But a person's age, ethnicity, and gender simply do not cut it as warning signs. Every time your unthinking prejudice makes me or anyone else an involuntary representative of scariness, you hurt the feelings — and raise the blood pressure — of a human being who deserves better. You become, in effect, an unwitting apostle for some of the more boorish beliefs burdening our planet. This is antisocial behavior at its worst. Change it.

If you're a white person, and find yourself persona non grata on a largely black bus or train route, with passengers emitting potently noxious signals for your benefit, you should try, like young black males caught in such social ambushes, to treat this as you would any other bizarre compulsion. You can defend yourself, if you choose, by preemptively guarding the empty seat beside you. But such petty relief is strictly stopgap. Are you really willing to play cat-and-mouse on buses and trains forever? Better, in the end, for you to understand what looms behind the rage: a siege mentality to which many African Americans have succumbed, one in which they judge all whites as broadly and as harshly as they themselves feel judged. You, as a white person, can escape abuse by getting off the bus. For black Americans, it is not so easy.

Survival Suggestions

1. If you are targeted for ethnic avoidance, take the clinical view.

Spare your cardiovascular system and try to shed the aggravation. Folks who treat you in this way are in the throes of a kind of casual madness. Let them dance around and expend their energy this way if they like. Meanwhile, you can sit and ride unencumbered by such baggage.

2. If you target others for ethnic avoidance, quit it.

Pay attention to your habits. This is not some trivial matter of "political correctness." You can dismiss it as such if you're not up to the challenge of behaving like a civilized human being. But if you are serious about wanting to treat other people fairly, you will not allow yourself to routinely diss people who deserve better from you.

Matters of Opinion

6

Rage Radio and Screaming Heads: How to Survive Talk Show Culture

They are 12 percent of the population. Who the hell cares?

— Rush Limbaugh, syndicated radio host, replying to a caller who said blacks deserve greater attention

I've been to Africa three times. All right? You can't bring Western reasoning into the culture. The same way you can't bring it into fundamental Islam.

— Bill O'Reilly, Fox News Network personality

I can tell which ones don't need to be looked at [as terrorism risks], I can tell you that. Old ladies, old black men, little children, blondes, blue eyed.

— Ann Coulter, commentator

They've got a big target on there, ATF. Don't shoot at that, because they've got a vest on underneath that. Head shots, head shots. . . . Kill the sons of bitches.

— G. Gordon Liddy, Watergate conspirator and radio host, advising his listeners on what to do if armed agents of the Bureau of Alcohol, Tobacco, and Firearms tried to disarm them

You should only get AIDS and die, you pig.

— Michael Savage, responding to an unfriendly caller

"W hat's wrong with having a little personality on the air?" some might ask. "So the commentators get excited. So they're opinionated. So what? It's entertaining. It's free speech. What's the harm?"

Well, the harm, actually, is that much of this prime- and drive-time free speech has become a license to lie. Limbaugh, O'Reilly, and Coulter, in particular, are notorious for making inflammatory statements that are flat-out untrue. Limbaugh, for instance, asserted on the air in 1994 that there was no proof that nicotine was addictive[1] — an interesting bit of denial given his own later struggle with prescription drug addiction. These three bellicose personalities alone have spawned a cottage industry in published and online research debunking their fictional claims.[2]

Moreover, this kind of "he who shouts first and accuses the most wins" hollering has arguably injected more stupidity and abject political ignorance into Americans' public consciousness than any other media influence in recent decades.

Here's how bad this has become: a recent study by the Program on International Policy Attitudes at the University of Maryland compared Americans' media habits with their knowledge of world affairs related to the Iraq War. The findings were stunning. During the run-up to the U.S. invasion of Iraq and in subsequent months, a substantial proportion of Americans held three blatant misperceptions about the war and world opinion. Sixty-eight percent believed that Iraq played a key role in September 11. Thirty-four percent continued to erroneously believe that weapons of mass destruction had been found even after this had been publicly disproved. And 31 percent held the grossly mistaken belief that most of the world backed the American invasion, while another 31 percent believed, also wrongly, that world opinion was evenly split.

But here is the study's blockbuster finding: viewers of Fox News Network were significantly likelier to hold these misperceptions than viewers or listeners of any other major network — nearly four times as likely as the audience for NPR/PBS, which ranked as the best-informed audience in the study. Even more profoundly, the study found that *viewers' misperceptions increased in proportion to the frequency with which they watched Fox.*[3]

In other words, to paraphrase a quip I once heard from comedian and Fox critic Al Franken: the more you watch Fox, with its bombastic pundits and drama-laden coverage, the less you know.

I will offer you a personal plan of counterattack to such revved-up disinformation a few pages from now. But first, let's look at how we reached this sorry state of high-pitched, low-quality so-called news in the first place.

Whatever your opinion about the mass media, one thing on which we can all agree is that American journalism and commentary are now overwhelmingly corporate entities, run by huge conglomerates according to corporate priorities. It was not always this way. Since the 1980s, mega-mergers driven by major shareholders' and CEOs' hunger for greater profits have steadily concentrated the ownership of American media. Today, a handful of massive corporations own the vast majority of print and electronic media outlets through which most Americans receive their news and information.

A twenty-first-century publicly traded conglomerate that owns food, clothing, and media companies is run very differently than a mid-twentieth-century family-owned newspaper or stand-alone television network. It's not that we can look back on some lost gilded age of journalistic purity; the business of American mass media has never been free of greedy scoundrels. But up until the merger mania took hold, there were at least certain bedrock assumptions about the public good that were widely shared among news publishers and networks. It was broadly understood that ownership of a major news medium carried with it at least minimal responsibilities for independence, investigative initiative, and resistance to intimidation by government or advertisers. Such ethics made a story such as Watergate — in which two *Washington Post* reporters brought down the Nixon White House — possible. I question whether today's crop of corporate-groomed journalists would even be capable of breaking such a story.

Moreover, television journalism now overwhelmingly dominates the news industry, far surpassing print as the medium that today's Americans turn to for daily information. And today's broadcast news industry, driven by the profit-centered directives of trustees and managers of large parent corporations rather than the needs of past owners who felt more of a personal stake in public-interest journalism, has developed a formula for success: cut out the most expensive elements of news gathering, and instead milk emotion and personality for all they're worth in choosing stories and on-air personalities.

Massive corporations that insist on inflexible profit margins for their subsidiaries are very bad at covering news in any depth or with any variety — because it is much cheaper to cover a narrower range of political players and issues and to count on spectacular events such as plane crashes and disasters and scandals to boost ratings. True journalism is, after all, expensive: it requires a large number of reporters, who in turn require a lot of time and expense to go out and painstakingly hunt down stories of public importance.

But McJournalism, in which reporters simply report the facts of sensational events or merely quote the statements of officials (often offering a "battle of quotes" for contrast rather than daring to independently investigate the evidence) is much cheaper. And more profitable. And so is McCommentary, the current host-driven model wherein a single supercharged on-air pundit attracts huge audiences and advertising revenues through sheer force of personality.

Enter the Attack Host.

For centralized corporate news operations, this idea is a golden goose: put a polarizing personality in front of a camera or a microphone and let him rant, snort, accuse, and abuse his way to fabulously profitable notoriety. There is only one principal actor to pay — albeit exorbitantly — instead of an entire raft of players. And what he says almost doesn't matter as long as it stops short of offending corporate interests or spurring mass outrage. What matters is that it have *juice:* a raw, preferably angry edge that keeps audiences coming back for their daily hit of righteous indignation. Sympathetic audiences are led to feel like victims and rebels. Dissenters are met with ridicule and contempt. Slurs and insults fly. The decibel level rises. And standards for truth-telling evaporate as hosts such as Limbaugh and O'Reilly learn that they can get by on raw audacity, spouting untruths with such vitriolic brazenness that others hesitate to question them.

What we end up with is the "SHUT UP!" reflex: the reduction of discourse to a kind of personal fascism whereby one either crushes or is crushed, humiliates or is humiliated. With such high stakes for winning arguments, there is no place in the conversation for true equality or give-and-take. And that is why virtually all such Rage Talk hosts fight dirty. They screen callers for favorable points of view. They cut off those who challenge them. They either work alone, monopolizing the line of discussion, or offer "balance" by having lower-wattage cohosts with differing points of view who will allow themselves to be bullied by the dominant host. The on-air guest lists are heavily weighted toward political allies, with only an occasional fiery opponent allowed to share the spotlight.

After more than a decade of such shows, the classic model, in the Rush Limbaugh/Bill O'Reilly mold, is now to have an in-your-face right-wing host entertaining the faithful with diatribes aimed at nonbelievers. For variety, some, such as Fox's *Hannity and Colmes,* offer an acquiescent liberal as a cohost or as a safely manageable regular guest. Aggressively liberal or progressive guests are greeted with guns blazing, so that any conversation is more noise than interchange.

Gun-shy mainstream reporters are fond of passing off talk show culture as having "equal" abusiveness among hosts on both the political right and the left. But research as well as even the most casual observation refutes this convenient claim. There is no commentator on the left — none whatsoever — who is both as prominent and as outrageously abusive as Ann Coulter. Michael Moore doesn't come close; even his most provocative comments come nowhere near the recklessness of Coulter, who has called for all Arabs to be spied on, liberals to be sent to Guantanamo prison camp, and flesh-shredding "daisy-cutter" bombs to be wantonly dropped throughout the Middle East.[4] Nor is there a radio lefty with both the high profile and the monstrous persona of G. Gordon Liddy, who, as previously cited, has called for "head shots" in assassinating government agents. To be sure, there are crazies on both the left and the right. But the lefty crazies are relegated to the media margins, while the righty nutcases are squarely in the mainstream.

The annual assessment of the "100 Most Important Talk Show Hosts in America" by *Talkers Magazine,* the most prominent professional journal in the talk radio industry, sheds more light on this rightward tilt. In the magazine's 2006 list of the industry's leading radio hosts (also known as the "Heavy Hundred," ranked by stated criteria that included impact, longevity, ratings, revenue, and talent), the top five were, in order: Howard Stern, Rush Limbaugh (who was number one in the General Issues/Political Talk category), Sean Hannity, Michael Savage, and Dr. Laura Schlessinger. All, with the exception of Stern, are hard-core inflammatory conservatives; Stern, for his part, is simply inflammatory, but by no means a liberal. Of the list's top ten, at least seven are clear conservatives. The top one hundred list also includes, farther down, a smattering of liberals, including Randi Rhodes and Al Franken. But the trend is clear.[5]

We know that money is what drives this noisy talk show machinery. But wherein lies the appeal of all of this right-wing shrieking and bawling? Yes, resentful whites with lousy (or no) jobs are easy marks for demagogic avengers with microphones. But I think there is something more going on here, having to do with national identity, and NPR radio personality Garrison Keillor put his finger on it in a 2005 essay: "The reason you find an army of right-wingers ratcheting on the radio and so few liberals is simple: Republicans are in need of affirmation, they don't feel comfortable in America and they crave listening to people who think like them. Liberals actually enjoy living in a free society; tuning in to hear an echo is not our idea of a good time."[6]

*   *   *

I think Keillor is onto something. When you think about it, beneath their bellicose pieties about the glories of the homeland and its God-given destiny, many of today's resentful American right-wingers actually loathe their country. They may crave the fictional nation of their myths and fantasies. But they loathe their actual nation, this place where they in fact live. It is a place that was occupied by other people first and is now home to an entire planet's worth of humans who bring all of their histories and hungers and gods and nongods to bear in a beautiful riot of coexistence. But some Americans hate this. They hate the fact that their neighborhoods keep changing, and that they have to keep adjusting to new accents and new customs and evolving ideas of what is fair and just. These fearful and angry would-be patriots may be fond of talking about democracy, but they are often not interested in living it. What they want is to be in charge. It curdles their blood that their assurance of getting their way is obstructed by the demographic facts and the (theoretical) principles of their nation. Every day while they lock their car doors against scary strangers and turn to Rush Limbaugh for sour radio comfort, they resent the real America.

So is it any wonder they can be so mean? So insecure? So needy?

Not long ago I was sitting in a small quick-copy shop waiting for my order. A fifty-ish white man, apparently a regular customer, strolled in and, after a minute of small talk at the counter, launched loudly into what I took to be his ritual rant in the general direction of the clerk about 9/11, the "lefty food police" and their persecution of McDonald's, and his own well-planned regimen to protect his family from the imminent threat of terrorist attack.

I found myself staring at him, wondering what would possess a grown man — aside from the obvious ailment of overexposure to the Fox Network — to behave so antisocially in a store among strangers. Why was he driven to so feverishly intrude upon other people's aural space with this personal show of outrage?

Then it hit me: He doesn't feel at home here. In this store. In this city. In America. And he's doing what bitter orphans everywhere do: telling the fearsome and unwelcoming world, at every personal opportunity, to go to hell.

By the standards of reason it is certifiably loony: a middle-aged white man, who by both ethnicity and gender is part of the single most privileged group of humans on the planet, convincing himself that he and his kind are hapless pariahs who are being shoved off the edge of the earth by the real power elite — the liberals and the blacks and the gays. If you're laughing, I don't blame you.

It is both ironic and tragic: this right-wing faction of scared and angry mostly white Americans, estranged from their natural allies of working- and middle-class Americans of color, clasping their Rush-blaring radios like pacifiers while the corporations that sponsor the furious noise quietly pillage their nation's tax revenues and flush working families' economic security down the toilet.

Meanwhile, all of us pay a personal as well as a political price for this kind of public speech.

You know the feeling: You are forced to listen to some radio talk show host raving while you sit in a waiting room, and you feel the bile rise in you as heads in the room nod at his nonsensical arguments. You are afraid to mention anything even remotely political around casual acquaintances, not just because it's impolite but because it could open up enough pent-up ugliness to spoil an event or alter a relationship. You feel much of everyday political interchange closed off to you, except for commiseration with people with whom you already agree, because of the harsh punishment for disagreement. Your radio stops momentarily on the whining of yet another wronged right-winger, and your hand leaps to change the station before your blood pressure rises.

This personalizing of political conflict — treating issues as a theater of personal abuse on the air — locks both listeners and nonlisteners into airtight rooms that offer only frustration as a release. One cannot talk to those on the "wrong" side of the issue because they are the enemy, the anti-Americans, the idiots, the whatever. And yet one cannot peacefully endure the tension of feeling so put-upon and so misunderstood by "the other."

The lucrative poison of McCommentary has managed to shut down the most essential of human interchanges: arguing toward understanding. As a result, everyone's personal plumbing is now clogged. No wonder everyone is mad.

But it doesn't have to be this way, at least not for you.

Consider the following suggestions for surviving talk show culture on a daily basis.

Survival Suggestions

1. Give yourself a break and turn off the Attack Host blather.

Just turn it off. It's bad for your blood pressure. It's bad for your sense of self because it distorts your place in the world;

what an angry talk show host does best is make listeners feel powerless so that the host can offer himself as their champion. It's also bad for your community because it shuts down openings for conversation; everyone is too enraged, or too afraid, to talk politics. So ditch the Rage Talk habit. And let them sell helplessness to someone else. You'll feel better.

2. Understand that Rage Talk does not reflect what Americans really want.

McCommentary is like doughnuts or heroin — a concoction that creates an immediate habit without any consideration for the long term. Think of talk show culture as a short-term fatty opiate that is all about the now: the quickly satisfying hit of smugness and sarcasm, the self-esteem-boosting indulgence in a sense of superior morality and patriotism, the self-lionizing exaggeration of the evils posed by those who disagree with you. Consider, most of all, the ample profits enjoyed by the conglomerates that hawk this brand of opinionated junk from franchised stations across the nation.

Look closely and you'll see that right-wing Rage Radio carefully swings the attention of emotionally frayed working Americans away from the things they most deeply want, while substituting instead a kind of "power through contempt" that can leave an underpaid and non-health-insured listener feeling strength in his rage at narrowly targeted others: foreigners, college professors, feminists, liberals, people of color, women, people critical of the establishment. Note, as well, that the targets of this choreographed rage are never those at the heart of the establishment: corporations, health-insurance CEOs, the wealthy citizens who benefit most from tax cuts, major shareholders whose decisions slash workforces and wages and benefits for the hyped-up callers who jam conservative talk show phone lines.

What right-wing talk show culture amounts to, then, is a cleverly machined redirecting of the anger of America's working and middle classes away from the logical targets of their rage and toward, instead, easily hyped cultural and ethnic targets who serve to preoccupy audiences while corporate and establishment looting of the public trust continues undisturbed. Understand this, and you will be less intimidated by the right-wing media noise machine. It needs to make so much noise precisely to drown out the arguments that would (and eventually will) draw its audiences toward the forbidden issues of economic and social fairness.

3. Take heart in the fact that Rage Talk culture is self-limiting.

It is, actually, unsustainable. No one can lie forever and get away with it; sooner or later the economic and political facts of American life will reveal themselves no matter how stridently right-wing pundits continue to make excuses for the status quo.

4. Fight it with specifics.

As I have said, much of Rage Talk gets by on raw audacity. Fire-breathing hosts lie and mislead with impunity because potential critics are afraid of them. Call the bluff. Go to the Web sites that research these hosts' many errors (do a search-engine inquiry for any major right-wing host and literally hundreds of critical sites will appear). Sift through them for the sites that are well documented and well reviewed. Then put the information to work: call the show and challenge the host, write a letter, or contact reporters who cover media. The fact is, most of these hot-air purveyors can't stand the heat when you turn it on.

5. Resist the intrusion of Rage Radio and TV into public space.

Do not accept the presumption that this *Pravda*-like braying is acceptable in shared space. Ask the hotel lobby clerk or the airport bartender or the waiting-room receptionist to change the channel. Let them know that, as with the prattle of loudmouthed cell phone users, you will not accept this rubbish being forced into your space. And as a last resort, keep an iPod and headphones handy.

6. Combat it in your own personal media diet.

Give yourself the benefit of an antidote, namely counterbalancing media consumption. NPR, although increasingly softened up by right-wing pressure, remains a broad-minded alternative to the commercial networks. The Pacifica and Air America radio networks provide progressive voices. European and other foreign media (e.g., the BBC) offer coverage of world news not afflicted with the American-friendly slant of most of our nation's corporate media. Knowing that you have global companionship in your nonenraged and nuanced sense of the world goes a long way toward daily peace.

7. Shrug off the absurd notion that questioning a person's ideas equals challenging her personhood.

As you go about your daily encounters with people, do not buy into the packaging of politics as personal warfare. It is a harmful product created to help the news and entertainment industry to make a lot of money. It bears no relation to real life and real democracy. In a true democracy, people with conflicting ideas are not out to destroy or humiliate one another. They are, on the contrary, out to struggle their way toward some better way of getting along — precisely because they cannot escape one another. In our case, we all live in a common house known as the United States of America. If you want to do something really patriotic, go out and talk excitedly about issues, and ask questions, and raise objections to points of view that do not make sense to you. But do this in a way that allows you the possibility of changing your mind or learning something, and that enables you to *continue to coexist with the rest of us the next day.*

Make no mistake: despite their America-first rhetoric, the Rage Talk bullies do not believe in the democratic exchange of ideas. They believe in getting their way. Toward that end, they will lie. They will cheat. They will shout you down. They will annihilate opponents. They will do whatever it takes. You might feel all right about this for the moment if they happen to be on your side of some issue or other. But *what's going to happen to you when they're not?* That is the question to ponder.

Instead of pursuing the politics of personal warfare, start pursuing the politics of respectful struggle. Do that, and you will never again have to apologize for disagreeing with anyone.

7

Take Me to Your Leader: Who Gets to Speak for Whom?

t is a title conferred every day upon individual members of ethnic groups without their permission: "Ambassador for Your People." It bestows the ostensible responsibility upon a person, anytime and anywhere, to enlighten well-intentioned others about the alleged point of view of "their" people — as in, "Why do so many of your people feel that — ?" or "What is your people's opinion of — ?" The topic could be anything, but it often reflects the questioner's stereotyped view of that group: interrogating an Asian-American seatmate about raising smart or talented children, quizzing a black passenger about Bill Cosby's controversial comments about the black urban poor.

From the questioner's standpoint, this is all perfectly innocent; when you have few or no friends of that particular ethnic background and little understanding of the range of realities of their lives, you open whatever windows you can. And who better to ask for information than one of "them"?

But that's the problem: You are asking one person, with one set of experiences, one heart, and one brain. Here she is, minding her own business on a plane or at work, and suddenly she is asked to step in for millions of "her" folk. The temptation is to snap, "Why are you asking *me?*"

Look, it's not wrong for a well-meaning person to seek out another person's opinion. It's wrong, though, to treat that opinion as anything other than one person's view. The unspoken assumption behind a what-do-you-people-think interrogation ("One opinion from your group is the same as any other, so I'll ask you") is aggravating beyond belief. Imagine the gall of, say, a foreigner asking a white American "how white people feel" about antipoverty programs. *Which* white people? Those staffing food kitchens for homeless families? Those playing golf with owners of sweatshops? Those wearing swastikas? We take it for granted as a nation that there are hundreds of millions of ways of being white. Well, then, the same truth applies to everybody else.

I will speak here about what I know from my experience — being treated by acquaintances as a "black ambassador" — but clearly this is a problem that people of all ethnicities encounter, and the same solutions apply.

Forget entirely about gaining any kind of broad knowledge about black folk, or any other folk, from talking with one or two people. There are no shortcuts. If you want to know what one black friend thinks about something, ask him. If you want to know what a lot of black people think, ask a lot of black people. And if you really want to know how deep and how wide the river of discourse runs, check out the world of African-American books, magazines, journals, newspapers, Web sites, and television and radio programs. From the magazine *Ebony*, for instance, you might conclude that all African Americans worship celebrity and aspire to become middle managers for large corporations. From the Nation of Islam newspaper, the *Final Call*, you might think that all black people study African languages, eschew pork, and embrace Islam. From Ward Connerly's book *Creating Equal: My Fight Against Race Preferences*, you might infer that all black Americans are against affirmative action. None of these generalizations, of course, is true. How could *any* such sweeping statements be true?

I have black friends who, to this day, when cornered to defend some blanket statement that they have made about white people, will say, "Oh, come on. You know how *they* are." But I do not know how "they" are. Neither do you, nor do any of us. On that score, it should already be clear to us that the race card is a useless guide for feeling out someone you do not know well, particularly since many of our experiences as blacks with well-meaning white questioners have revealed just how shallow a range of human perspectives some whites attribute to "us": crime, affirmative action, crime, celebrities, crime, sports, crime.

Years ago, I gave a poetry reading at which the white hostess introduced me to the mostly white crowd as a poet who would bring into the room "the black man's angry rhythms of the street" or some such patronizing nonsense. I had no idea who she was talking about. I proceeded, through my poems, to present a clearer vision of my land-scape, which includes wind-scoured Alaskan tundra as well as steaming pavement, and in which I have furiously slaughtered fish with my father as well as gratefully smiled at a passing church lady. My hostess let on to no disap-pointment, but I am certain that she, having clearly taken only a cursory look at my work, had been expecting some spokesman for Authentic Black Urban Angst rather than an actual human being. I was, after all, black, male, and wearing jeans. What else was there for her to know?

The epitome of this kind of blunder is the way in which many whites view black celebrities. Through the "black ambassador" treatment, Condoleezza Rice, a Bush administration figure and former Chevron Oil trustee with political views significantly to the right of what polls show most black Americans believe, becomes a "black figure" whose opinions are deemed important for race relations. Jesse Jackson, a venerable and eloquent black activist all his life, becomes a reference point (particularly on the far right, where commentators are fond of mocking his preachy speech) for "what blacks are saying." Barack Obama, a rel-ative political newcomer with both strong opinions and broad personal and political appeal, becomes the potential "face of a new black leadership."

One celebrity who in recent years seems to have out-maneuvered this "black icon" label is Oprah Winfrey, a woman of dazzling presence and even more dazzling wealth. Although her personal dramas (for instance, her being locked out of an exclusive Paris shop) can still become flash points for explosive racial issues, she is, on the whole, far more a human figure than a racial one. She did not, for instance, take on the cattle industry as a black woman; she took them on as an antidisease advocate, period. Her fans, of all ethnicities, love her not because she is black, but because she is Oprah. The same universal glamour applies to Michael Jordan and some other black celebrities.

Still, some whites have a tendency (perhaps without even knowing it) to try to entrap black celebrities, or the black woman across the hall, into speaking for all black Americans at moments of racial doubt. And despite blacks' disproportionately greater exposure to a variety of white opinions, some blacks persist in treating whites the same way. In either case, it is a losing proposition: little knowledge gained, much ignorance preserved.

Whatever my color, whatever my heritage, it comes down to this: Want to know what I think? Ask me and I'll tell you. Want to know what all "people like me" think? Forget it. End of conversation.

Survival Suggestions

1. Don't even think about asking somebody what "people like them" think.

It is insulting beyond belief and will gain you, at best, one person's opinion, and at worst, an awkward and painful encounter with an offended person.

2. This doesn't mean you shouldn't ask for people's opinions.

Asking a person what she thinks about something, in a way that makes it clear you are interested in her personal point of view, is part of normal conversation. Of course you should show interest, if the conversation seems to lead comfortably toward matters of opinion (and that may be a big "if"). But the key, again, is for you to show interest in the actual individual rather than in her membership in a group whose "point of view" you seek. Approach anyone so rudely, and you'll pretty much deserve what you get.

3. If you are treated as an ambassador, make it a teachable moment.

There is usually no need to respond with outright unkindness; inquisitors usually mean well, and it's not as if they are calling you a bad name or actively expressing some vile stereotype (if they are, that is another matter entirely). But nonetheless, correction is called for. Let them know why their line of questioning is not appreciated.

Five minutes after he met me at a gathering, the white father of a friend of mine suddenly pulled me aside and asked me my position on Bill Cosby's remarks about the black poor. I told him, in two sentences, that I was one black man and not 13 million, and that in any case I hadn't come there to discuss race and Cosby and I didn't feel like talking about it. End of inquisition. Another tactic is to turn the tables and ask, "What do *you people* think about such-and-such?" which pretty well makes the point. Be creative about it. But do not submit to ambassadorship. It is an impossible job, and it feeds habits of thought that we need to eradicate.

8

Till O. J. Do Us Part: Race and Our Encounters with Police

*T**he police. Charged with serving, protecting, and occasionally ticketing. Their job is to keep an eye out for trouble in your neighborhood. Or maybe, if you're black, to keep an eye out for you in neighborhoods where they think you don't belong. The police. They hand you a traffic summons and tell you to have a nice day. Or maybe, if you're black, they whale on you with nightsticks, kick you into a fetal ball, and then order you to stand up. The police. They respond to our calls and retrieve our stolen cars and maintain what's left of the peace. Or maybe, if you're black, they keep you perched alertly on your tailbone when you catch that glint of blue or red flashing in your rearview mirror.*

And maybe, if you're an Arab American, they follow you and watch your habits. Or they enter you into a database that federal agencies can later use to secretly detain you or "render" you to a nation that practices torture. Or they keep you feeling just plain wary and watchful when you wish you didn't have to be.

It's crazy, think some whites: all these African Americans with their preconditioned rage toward the police, who, nonetheless, look after the property and safety of black folks, too. It's crazy, think some blacks: all of these whites living in utter denial of the spectacular brazenness with which police reserve special scrutiny — and abuse — for black people. It's crazy, think some Arab Americans and defenders of civil liberties: an entire society gone terrorism-mad, expending its energy where it does unconscionable harm to the innocent while doing little or nothing to reduce true threats.

Well, somebody's crazy.

What's crazy is our society's smug civic pretense of a single standard of law enforcement when in fact we have many. Ask the families of young black women who disappear without a trace if they receive anything like the high-octane law enforcement and media campaigns that often follow the cases of young blond white women in comparable circumstances. Ask black males who drive expensive cars, or who drive, period. Ask Arab Americans who travel often by air.

Much of what I will say here pertains to the specific dynamic of black versus white experience because it is what I am in the best position to understand and describe. But I am aware, and perhaps you are, too, that many of the same principles of this hypocrisy apply, with different and sometimes much more horrific results, to the standards by which many Arab Americans have been scrutinized and judged since September 11, 2001. Here we are talking not only about harassment or excessive surveillance or beatings by police or unjust verdicts but about "disappearances" to secret overseas prisons and "rendition" of people, formally charged with no crimes, to nations that torture. It is a topic whose scope extends far beyond the reach of this book. Yet it must be a part of any serious discussion of the problems of current American law enforcement. For every element I describe in this chapter of the unique and embattled history of black/white issues of law enforcement, consider the equivalent, and sometimes more appalling, dramas now playing out daily in the treatment of Americans of Arab descent. These injustices require our fiercest attention and commitment for the same reasons that the black/white issues do: fair treatment, due process, human rights, and adherence to the Constitution.

In that sense, much of what I am about to present here about blacks and whites can and should be read as a broader call for awareness and justice.

When it comes to law enforcement, many blacks and whites still live on opposite sides of a practically impermeable divide. Call it the Melanin Curtain — a magically fluid but durable veil through which, say, a middle-class black woman browsing in a jewelry store can become, to the eye of a security guard, a smartly dressed thief. The same veil can make her white counterpart invisible, unworthy of notice. Whether it's a matter of traffic citations or felony arrests, the problem is not that blacks or whites as groups are lying when they recite contradictory histories of their treatment at the hands of police. The problem is that both are telling the truth.

If you are white, the first thing that you need to understand is that black people are not making this stuff up. You need to try to imagine living in a parallel universe in which much of the public invisibility that you and many other whites take for granted is denied. The racial double standard in law enforcement is not some self-excusing concoction of black Americans. It is as real as the sudden hook of a siren or a sudden yank at the neck. Get used to the idea: actual people in actual encounters with the law are seen and treated differently because of skin color, with a consistency etched in the research.

A 1999 Amnesty International report found that "in jurisdictions across the USA, the overwhelming number of victims of police brutality, unjustified shootings and deaths in custody are members of racial or ethnic minorities."[1] New York and Los Angeles have been notorious hotbeds of such incidents. The 2000 fatal shooting of unarmed black security guard Patrick Dorismond by a New York City police officer, for which the city paid Dorismond's family a $2.25 million settlement, and the 1991 videotaped beating of Rodney King by Los Angeles Police Department officers (more on this later) are two of the more egregious examples. But reports and community outrage concerning such incidents are all too common, from Virginia Beach to Baltimore to Cincinnati to Houston.

Most such abuse can be traced to a militarized police culture that began with the so-called War on Drugs, known by some African Americans as the "War on Blacks," since it has driven officers to vehemently target black communities for drug arrests with an intensity entirely disproportionate to true demographic patterns of drug use. According to a 1999 American Civil Liberties Union (ACLU) report, blacks make up 13 percent of America's drug users, 37 percent of those arrested on drug charges, 55 percent of those convicted, and 74 percent of drug offenders sentenced to prison. This despite the fact that government statistics reveal that 80 percent of America's cocaine users are white, and the average cocaine user is a middle-class white suburbanite, according to the report.[2]

What has taken hold is a self-fulfilling police culture of imbalanced drug scrutiny. The ACLU report explains its genesis this way:

> Racial profiling is based on the premise that most drug offenses are committed by minorities. The premise is factually untrue, but it has nonetheless become a self-fulfilling prophecy. Because police look for drugs primarily among African Americans and Latinos, they find a disproportionate number of them with contraband. Therefore, more minorities are arrested, prosecuted, convicted, and jailed, thus reinforcing the perception that drug trafficking is primarily a minority activity. This perception creates the profile that results in more stops of minority drivers. At the same time, white drivers receive far less police attention, many of the drug dealers and possessors among them go unapprehended, and the perception that whites commit fewer drug offenses than minorities is perpetuated. And so the cycle continues.[3]

The report goes on to cite a 2001 Gallup poll showing that 55 percent of whites and 83 percent of blacks believe racial profiling is widespread.[4] Maryland, Connecticut, and Rhode Island, for example, have come under fire for persistent racial profiling of motorists. There are, of course, anecdotes by the thousands in which drivers of color tell of being selectively pulled over, handcuffed, detained, subjected to car searches, or otherwise treated as suspect by police with no demonstrable justification. These human targets cover the entire socioeconomic spectrum, from movie stars to politicians to ordinary working people.

I have a profiling story of my own. At a major metropolitan train station some years ago, after returning home from a business trip to New York, I was surrounded and quizzed by white undercover detectives to whom I appeared to "fit the profile" — their words — for drug trafficking. When I took my complaint to the city's black chief prosecutor, he sighed. He was familiar with the clash between overwhelmed detectives and the rights of citizens. He told me his own stories about having been repeatedly stopped and questioned while in college and law school by white police officers who found him "suspicious." He was more than just sympathetic. He was upset by my allegations, and promised to investigate and to push the chief of police into demanding that detectives exhibit more judicious behavior. The prosecutor (he later become mayor) kept his word. As part of the fallout from my case, the (black) supervisor of the three detectives came to my office and, to my surprise, personally apologized.

Chances are that within a week or two another law-abiding black person was accosted by the same detectives.

Apologies are well and good for those fortunate enough to have contacts (a friend was an assistant prosecutor in this city), but the fact remains that in spite of President George W. Bush's highly publicized statements criticizing racial profiling, the U.S. Supreme Court has condoned the constitutionality of using profiles to stop and search people. Every day countless black citizens who, like everyone, want the simple freedom to move unmolested in public are detained and interrogated by police — not because they fit the description of a particular suspect, but because they look to police like the kinds of people who might turn out to be suspects. Which is to say, black.

In the 1990s, the ACLU filed a class-action lawsuit on behalf of minority motorists detained by the Maryland State Police along Interstate 95. The suit grew out of a 1993 lawsuit on behalf of a Harvard-educated black lawyer and his family, who for no apparent reason were stopped and searched on the highway. The ACLU alleged a long-term pattern of discrimination in racial profiling by state police. According to the police department's own figures for a three-year period, more than 75 percent of drivers stopped and searched on Interstate 95 were African Americans or members of other minority groups. If you are white, you may find such numbers surprising. If you are black, you probably won't.

But it's not just a male thing. Ask black women, many of whom who have received years, even decades, of jail time for such minor drug infractions as being in the car with someone who carried drugs. Ask black women about being watched and followed in stores. Some fight back. My favorite such story comes from a middle-class black woman: After being followed in an upscale store, she went to the counter as if to make a purchase but then instead loudly ordered the manager to cancel her charge account and told him why.

I am not saying that a black person should be excused from justified suspicion. But the justification should be one's actions, not one's race. When I was in college, several classmates and I, all black, made it a habit to steal anything we could get our hands on from a nearby convenience store. We were never caught. We wore long coats and walked out of the store with boxes of doughnuts, loaves of bread, six-packs of soft drinks. We didn't steal because we couldn't afford food. We stole because, as budding college radicals, we fancied ourselves to be striking small blows against capitalist authority. Did we deserve suspicion? Would we have deserved to be treated like thieves on the basis of our actions? Absolutely. But we deserved it no more than a certain white friend of mine. He was the first expert shoplifter I ever met.

When it comes to race, one's economic class, normally an effective American trump card (it might insulate a wealthy white suburbanite from such police crudities as public handcuffing or pistol-whipping), is often useless. Viewed through the Melanin Curtain, even a prosperous black person at certain moments has only one personal asset: blackness. "Just-another-nigger" stories crowd the landscape. Legendary jazz musician Miles Davis remained bitter until his death about the frequency with which California police pulled him over in his Ferrari for questioning, even when he *wasn't* speeding, as he liked to do. News accounts (often carried only in the black press) surface regularly of well-known black figures skirmishing with police officers who mistook them for "ordinary" (i.e., criminal) black folk in wealthy environs. The story about an unadorned Oprah Winfrey being denied entry to an exclusive shop in France, while not a police matter, struck for many blacks a familiar nerve of stereotype and exclusionism. For every such brightly lit racial story in Paris or Beverly Hills, there are a thousand more that take place in the nation's shadows.

Which brings us to the most notorious crucible ever for the clash of white and black ideas about police: the murder trial of O. J. Simpson.

The O. J. case is where black and white views of police went to war. We can argue forever about whether O. J. did it or not. Those who believe he was guilty can forever express shock over the jury's stunning ability to ignore overwhelmingly incriminating evidence. Those who think he was innocent can endlessly proclaim that the evidence was fixed and the prosecution tainted. But as an explanation of the verdict and its aftermath, such righteous fury completely misses the point. The storm over the trial was about something much deeper than one man's innocence or guilt. The real meaning of the O. J. trial for many blacks who fervently wished for his acquittal was not so much that they wanted him to win. It is that they wanted the police to lose.

Simpson's victory was due in part to legal genius, part to his goofy "good Negro" mega-celebrity, and part to prosecutorial weakness. But what really saved O. J. from life (or death) in the cell block was the Los Angeles Police Department's notorious legacy of racism — as supported by revelations about key officers in the trial — and the consuming desire in the African-American community for some kind of belated justice for the city's untold thousands of brutalized black men.

In the mere fact of being a prominent black male

murder defendant in a city with such a history, O. J. Simpson hit the jackpot. In the wake of the police beating of Rodney King, a black man, and the subsequent criminal acquittal of its videotaped perpetrators, no jury in Los Angeles with any black members was going to send this chuckling, amiable black football star to jail for life, whatever the evidence and whatever his history. Take it as a testament to the depth of black frustration that many African Americans chose so unlikely a beneficiary as O. J. Simpson — a man with little apparent attachment to any community of blackness — for their efforts.

If L.A. were an environment where blacks had a history of fair treatment by police, I would hazard to say that a guilty verdict for O. J. might have taken a jury an hour and caused a furor only among paparazzi, and King's videotaped beating by cops would have caused outrage but not outright insurrection. But instead, L.A.'s history has been one of abuse, graft, and injustice when it comes to the treatment of African-American citizens by the police. The ensuing rage has been palpable for many years. And so O. J. was "not guilty." And after the King videotape and verdict, L.A. was "suddenly" in flames. And countless white Americans were shocked, shocked at the bizarre behavior of those black folks.

And so, particularly if you are white, you need to realize that the world of many black Americans is one in which blue-uniformed people with guns can represent something shatteringly different from the world to which you may be accustomed. Some individual black people may crank up the volume on police villainy purely for personal or political effect, but the physical and psychological damage done by the double standard is as real as a corpse. Any honest racial conversation about the law has to begin here. If you are looking for truth, for some real understanding of what is happening racially when it comes to the law, you have to start listening to what black people are saying. This doesn't mean you have to buy every story, be it that of O. J. Simpson or anyone else. But it does mean that you must be open to truths that defy your own experience.

And if you are black, you need to recognize that most whites are not conspiring to deny the facts as you know them. They are not malevolently embracing a skewed view of the world, nor forcibly blinding themselves through sheer mean-spiritedness to the smoldering history between blacks and cops. Instead, most whites are like you: decent, well-intentioned people acting within the limitations of their own experience. Moreover, many poor whites know a great deal about the hard and ugly edge of the law. But the relatively insulated mass of white middle America has no direct knowledge of the dramas played out just offstage, beyond their peripheral vision. To them, your varied range of experience as a black person — particularly if you live in a low-income community — takes place in a void, somewhere beyond the edge of the earth, a place they can envision only through televised images, mostly of black criminals on the news and deeply tormented homicide detectives in serial dramas.

You needn't shoulder responsibility for widening such a white person's scope. You do, however, need to resist treating whites as mythical characters in their own right — as pernicious creatures of prejudice who hungrily collect and covet racial poisons, even as they cheer on the police. If you expect to be heard, you ought to treat people as if they are capable of listening.

Survival Suggestions

1. Understand that nobody here is lying.

With the exception of some Rage Talk pundits, politicians, and assorted petty hooligans, the whites and blacks who generally face off against each other with contradictory assessments of police are all telling the truth. And that's the problem: their experiences jarringly contradict one another. If you as a white person are to have a hope of being heard by blacks, you need to hear and accept the good-faith truths of black people's reporting of their experiences. And if you as a black person expect to be heard by whites who do not understand, you need to avoid the presumption that their lack of understanding is some ingrained or consciously embraced character flaw. Understand the power of pervasive misinformation. Expect (and demand) that whites be open to new information, just as you should demand it of yourself.

2. Take a stand.

Simply understanding that there is unfairness in police treatment is important. But it is not enough. Make your voice heard to local, state, and federal police and government authorities. And support organizations that document and work to end discriminatory treatment by police. The ACLU is one leading such group, but a basic Web search will yield many more.

3. Don't become a victim.

If you find yourself in what feels like a racially motivated situation with police, remember this: if in fact the cop is bigoted, he is probably also looking for an opportunity to accost or mistreat you in a way that he can later claim was provoked. Don't give it to him. Stay cool. Keep your hands in plain sight. Move and speak slowly and calmly. If you can, make a mental note of details, including his badge number, and if necessary advise him coolly that you are aware of your legal rights. Most important, remember that you can pursue a lawsuit or otherwise gain justice if you remain alive. But you can't if you're dead. I suggest, too, that you review the ACLU's "Know Your Rights: What to Do If You're Stopped by the Police," available at their web site as a downloadable PDF file that you can print and keep in your purse.[5]

9

The Extraterrestrial's Guide to Hate

I *'ll confess something: I have never really understood hate. Yes, I grew up in America. Yes, I have had epithets screamed at me from people in moving cars, witnessed — and been in — racial brawls, heard landlords lie through their teeth about vacancies, watched guys yank themselves away from an apparently good time with their friends in a bar simply to vent their fury at my very presence. I know rage and some of its sources: abuse, lost faith, broken promises, powerlessness. I know the drill on hate, and so perhaps do you. But somehow, I just can't envision being down in the works of the thing. Hate is such hard work. It is exhausting, punishing, and constant, an exercise in desperation and perennial defeat.*

I try to imagine what that must be like for a racist. I mean a serious *racist, someone who is sick with it, sour with it, like a razor-edged belch; someone who passes out pamphlets calling for a bloody end to this or that group; someone who chews constantly on his own anger; someone who feels perpetually threatened by racial enemies; someone who murders a complete stranger for the sake of a tattoo. What does such a person feel from the inside? What could congeal a soul in such a hellish state? I walk into a diner out in the country and see a white person turn away from a heaping plate of hot food to glare long and hard at me, and I wonder: What is it like, behind those hooded eyes, at the moment when the hated "other" looms in their field of vision?*

What was it like for those people in Rochester, New York — I don't know for certain who they were, but I have an idea — who signed the petition protesting my family's moving into our new house in a white neighborhood? What was it like to be that drunken white man in dirty clothes who thrust out his leg as if to trip me, a black stranger in a business suit, as I walked past him on a bus? What is it like for black kids who lie in wait to pummel any white stranger who happens to come along?

I don't know. Chances are, you don't either; if you did, you would not have this book in your hand; you would have flung it across the room, or, more likely, left it on the shelf. But I will tell you what we do know, you and I: we know that the anger thickens our very air in the places where we live. It crackles on car radios; it electrifies glares among strangers at malls; it forges our own shoulder-squaring readiness for ambush. We know, particularly in the fearful aftermath of 9/11, that strangers feel more and more like potential enemies. And we know that all of this leaves us less room, somehow, to move with ease, let alone joy.

Before my father suffered a crippling stroke, he had other ways of venting his rage. I remember the way that he had, when I was a child, of dealing with hateful white stares when we walked down a street. He would abruptly turn toward our scrutinizers and freeze, feet spread like a boxer's, hands on hips, eyes locked on the offending parties in a searing glare, as if to declare, "I stand to judge you." The watchers saw his defiance. What they did not see was the way that, at home, he cried.

Hate is a set of worming gears out there as big as the world. It constantly, mindlessly grinds at men and women regardless of skin color, reduces them to wounded flesh, spits them forth as skin desperadoes. And some of them want to hurt you, and others want to hurt me. They live among us and within us. Some carry live ammunition. How can we survive with our hearts intact?

It might help if we tried to see all of this from an alien's point of view. Say, a blue-skinned Venusian from a completely nonaggressive culture. Let's suppose that a series of seismic shifts is slowly but steadily lowering parts of the coastline of Venus's single continent into the ocean, gradually displacing hundreds of thousands into the already overcrowded interior. A treaty with the United States — which covets Venusian technological skills — allows some of these refugees to emigrate. With no room on Venus, they have little choice but to accept the offer of safe passage to America. But it means leaving the peace of

Venusian tradition — in which trust among complete strangers has been the norm for millennia — for an American way of life riddled with bizarre conflicts and fears. Chief among these, as blared in the Venusian tabloids, is the American spectacle of race.

In this new place where neither his azure skin nor his automatic empathy with strangers is taken in stride, the newly arrived Venusian is in dire need of sound advice. Fortunately, as part of the briefing process, a Venusian government committee of experts has prepared a series of handy brochures for prospective emigrants, including one on adapting to the racial biases of Americans. The Venusian gets his hands on a copy.

The Venusian's Guide, Vol. 24: Habits of Race in America

Welcome to Earth and its most aggressive culture, the United States. As part of your early adjustment, you MUST familiarize yourself with important rules governing the social behavior of Americans. In this pocket guide, you will find information that will help you to begin to understand and befriend Americans — a convivial people at heart — without falling victim to their chief weaknesses. READ THIS GUIDE. It will spare you painful — or dangerous — social errors.

Cardinal custom: Americans sort people by skin color, which they call "race." They base their reactions (warmth, hostility, trust, mistrust) to strangers not chiefly on behavior, but on skin hue and other "racial" traits. The prejudice has a pattern — the lighter the better (with some variations for hair, eyes, and facial features) — and the custom stems from a recent system of captive labor for profit, for which skin color was used as an explanation for enslavement. Many Americans remain vague about the facts of this enterprise; you will find the darkest-skinned Americans the most willing to discuss its peculiar history.

More recent events, involving an attack on certain shrines of American power, have also intensified and complicated Americans' skin-sorting customs, bringing in an additional obsession with "ethnicity," a broader form of categorization that can involve one's skin hue, culture, and nation of ancestry. We will summarize these developments shortly.

Prepare. Racial prejudice is unlike any custom you have ever encountered. It contradicts all of your instincts, as a Venusian, about what to expect from others. Among strangers in the United States, fear is the rule rather than warmth and trust (see vol. 9, *Property and Crime*), and race is its chief symbol. Despite your special citizenship under the Treaty, in informal interactions your blue skin may place you toward the bottom of the American skin scale. You will meet with suspicion in public places, be more carefully scrutinized during transactions, have more trouble renting or purchasing a dwelling, and often be feared in close contact.

You will find that Americans of all colors carry great tension over skin color. In its most destructive form, the tension explodes in an all-consuming bitterness toward others: hate. CAUTION: Hate is contagious. Allowed to run its course, it could sicken and kill you, or drive you to harm others. In your natural desire as a Venusian to be embraced — and your distress at being inexplicably spurned — you may be tempted to hate as well. Do not succumb. Instead, follow these three crucial directives to maintain emotional balance.

1. Immunize yourself.

In America, you will witness skin hate everywhere, even in places you would least expect to find it. You will be shocked. Thousands of crimes of racial hate are reported nationally each year, and many more go unreported. Hate organizations are active in all fifty regions of the nation. Hatred is expressed among all skin colors but appears to be keenest between the very light-skinned descendants of enslavers (immigrants from a continent known as Europe who are commonly referred to as "white") and the very dark-skinned descendants of the previously mentioned African slaves, commonly called "black." The hateful behaviors vary: people are attacked and killed, sometimes even castrated and hanged by the neck; places of worship burned; property defaced; telephone threats made; anger expressed in broadcast messages; customers refused service. Even children are ridiculed or treated with public cruelty due to skin color. Curiously, many Americans will share a home with a creature not of their species, yet refuse to inhabit space near a human of a different skin color.

You will wonder how such socially destructive behavior has survived. One reason is that slavery itself ended only recently, and its effects and attitudes persist. Another is that racism gives many (particularly the less prosperous among the whites) a delusion of power. A black family moving into a poor white area, for example, may be attacked by whites for "bringing down" the neighborhood. This is clearly senseless; the community's problem is poverty, not race. But feeling superior to blacks helps such whites to deny their own powerlessness.

Similarly, Americans are commonly willing to believe racial myths that an off-worlder can immediately recognize as nonsense. Not long ago in one American city, a white man murdered his female mate and claimed that a fictional black attacker committed the crime. Security forces conducted massive searches of black-occupied areas before the truth was revealed. In another instance, a white woman drowned her two children and blamed a nonexistent black lawbreaker for their disappearance. In both cases, whites uncritically accepted lies that appealed to popular suspicions about blacks. Some black Americans, for their part, embrace a creation myth in which whites are defined as the evil offspring of a wrongdoer.

More recent developments have heightened and complicated American's skin hate obsession. A demonically clever attack on the shrinelike structures housing the leadership of America's economic and military powers — using commandeered airborne vehicles containing American passengers — was successfully carried out by a group representing certain international resentments of America's domineering role on the planet. Americans, being prone to paranoia because they themselves gained their nation through conquest, slavery, and treachery, reacted with full-fledged panic and followed their leader at the time, an immature but highly persuasive figure, on a course of misdirected war and generalized fear and belligerence. The result was the hostile targeting — this time using ethnicity as a symbol for religion and culture — of certain generally brown-skinned so-called Arabic peoples linked by ancestry to a planetary region known as the Middle East, the general area from which the small group of above-mentioned attackers originated. Americans of Arab descent, virtually all of them innocent of any wrong-doing, have since been singled out for suspicion, abuse, attack, and in some cases detention and the barbaric infliction of pain and suffering, known as "torture." A broad and unreasoned fear of Arabic peoples remains high here, and persons with skin hues perceived as similar to theirs (a wide range from light tones to dark browns) or dressed in garments associated with Arabic traditions are often subjected to intense mistreatment.

Americans' bombardment of skin hate may make you feel vulnerable. Resist. Humans entertain skin hatreds due to feelings of being dominated. They lash out against imagined loss of power or security. If a skin-hater expresses animosity toward you, remember that he feels threatened by your presence, and he wants you to feel the same way. Your defensiveness serves, for him, as proof that his hostility has found its mark. He defines his image of himself, at least in part, by its relation to you. Do not grant him the same power.

Carefully observe a racist's glare. Your presence endangers, in his eyes, something he deems vital: job, stature, safety, national security, opportunity, fantasized superiority. His inflation of his own racial identity, and his denigration of yours, are attempts to restore lost confidence. Do not allow your self-regard to be wounded (and potentially contaminated) by race hate. Recognize, instead, that your Venusianity remains unshaken while the skin-hater's identity, always in need of reassurance, does not.

Remember: differences between individual Americans are always far greater than differences between ethnic groups — despite what many Americans themselves believe. In the contemporary United States, even some Venusians have been known to yield to the overwhelming pressure of racial hate. BE WARNED: If you surrender to the impulse to judge individuals by anything other than character, you will reach gravely erroneous conclusions. Such mistakes in threat detection can be costly; they can blind you to a human's actual intentions. Do not put yourself at risk.

2. Relearn self-defense.

What you have come to know on Venus as a normal state of awareness around strangers — a kind of relaxed attention — would be viewed by Americans as utter vulnerability to attack. This requires that you change your idea of self-defense. Americans, accustomed as they are to skin hate and to other fears of harm, believe that being constantly braced for invasion of one's person is normal. They accept low-grade, dormant fear as part of daily life, and they also accept its side effects, including numerous stress-related disorders and occasional violent outbursts by males.

Americans endure this from long habit. While you will find it strange and saddening, you will also discover that some individuals bear the stress better than others. Do not presume all Americans to have lost their capacity for joy and trust; you will deny

yourself opportunities for bonding. In seeking camaraderie or friendship, carry yourself with readiness
for conflict without being possessed by it. Walk
through a shopping arena or ride a group transportation device without displaying the "are-you-
looking-at-me" and "who-are-you" glances and
gestures that haunt the expressions of many light-
and dark-skinned Americans in public places. Resist
false prompts for combat. Then (as on Venus), on the
rare occasions when you must fight, you will feel
free do so, and justified in your self-defense.

3. Engage.

Skin-haters tend to avoid any personal contact with
the resented "other" that might change their beliefs.
At their most extreme, they not only dislike those
they have targeted, but also actively prevent themselves from liking them. They associate exclusively
with their "own kind," so that their only contact with
the "hated" skins is through physical attack or legal
procedure. This enables all such groups to hate symbols instead of hating actual humans. The cycle continues with the help of resentment bred by poverty,
international hostilities, and ongoing racial and ethnic discrimination.

    You will sometimes be frustrated by such
obstacles to emotional rapport. Proceed with care.
Hostilities in America have progressed to the point
where channels of communication taken for granted

among Venusians — such as the responsibility to both speak and listen face-to-face — are avoided by many due to mistrust and fear of bodily harm. An attempt to approach a skin-hater with an offer of civilized dialogue or personal openness can, in the wrong situation, cost you your life. You will no doubt observe, with some consternation, that such a demeanor among skin-haters only increases their own unhappiness. And you will find the resulting state of silent — or occasionally explosive — warfare to be hard to tolerate. You will need an intelligent way to approach such hazardous barricades.

The answer is to exercise engagement — to thoughtfully breach others' racial and ethnic barriers in those situations you judge yourself able to manage. As you encounter racial and ethnic misinformation or hostility in your everyday affairs of work and pleasure, you will face constant choices about whether, when, how, and with whom to personally engage on these matters. Expect no rules. Look, instead, for choices. Any action may be the right or wrong one.

> • In a drinking establishment, a man of one ethnicity allows himself to be drawn into conversation by an extremely large (and intoxicated) man of another ethnicity. The drunken man begins to make ill-advised comments about people of the other man's ancestry. The two men begin to argue, softly, then loudly. The smaller man wields the superior insult. The larger man wields the su-

perior punch to the jaw. The smaller man insti-
gates legal proceedings. The larger man is convicted of assault and sentenced to picking up
garbage in lieu of jail.

• A man is flagrantly denied an apartment
on the basis of skin color by the owner of a private dwelling. He has all that he needs to file a
lawsuit, including a witness, of a different race, to
whom the landlord offered the apartment the next
day. The man telephones the landlord. He tells her
his team is poised to sue her, and that it is an
open-and-shut case: she would be sure to lose.
But, he adds, he has far more important things to
do right now than to drag as sorry a creature as
she to court. He wants her to know, though, that
she has been caught, and that what she did was
wrong. She is flabbergasted. She stammers that
she meant no such thing. He tells her he knows
better. He tells her she will be watched. He tells
her to think about what she did. He tells her to
have a nice day.

• A man of a dark race decides to become
friendly with members of a white, skin-hating organization notorious, among other things, for
castrating dark-skinned men and hanging them
by the neck. The man has dinner with members of
this skin-hating group, talks with them, laughs
with them. He does this, he explains to an incredulous newspaper reporter, because he believes in
the raw power of dialogue. By popular standards,
he is crazy. But, he insists, that he and his new

friends are at least creating communication where none existed.

Ultimately, the decision about how to best respond to skin and ethnic hate must be yours. REMEMBER: Never fear options. Do not be caged by others' hostility. Be willing not only to confront, not only to defend, but also to engage in a manner that has personal effect. This may sometimes mean forcing recognition of a person's own hate back into their fiercely guarded space. Refuse to allow skin and ethnic haters to block the path of personal engagement. Choose carefully. But never relinquish the power to make choices.

May your journey bring fulfillment and prosperity.

10

Affirmative Action and Beyond: Controversies That Will Not Die, and Why

How to ensure, if you're white, that a black American will want to smack your face: *Remind her, whenever you have the opportunity, that no matter how hard she has strived, no matter how heroically her predecessors have sweated and bled and sacrificed, no matter how impressive her performance, no matter how wonderful her talents or accomplishments, an odor of suspicion will always hover over her achievements. Ask questions such as "You went to that school?" or "They gave you that job?" to reinforce the impression that a black person's competence is in need of verification. Suggest to black people that you understand, you really do, why an underqualified African American might seize*

119

upon affirmative action as a means of getting ahead, and why a black welfare mother might sit back comfortably and bear children at public expense. Above all, make it clear, through your own behavior as a white person, that an African American can expect to be routinely treated as a charity case and condemned to a lifetime of interrogation.

How to guarantee, if you're black, that a white American will want to turn on you with teeth bared: *Blame him, whenever possible, for the ongoing and gruesome mess begotten by white folks' original American sin: their barbaric behavior starting with their slave-owning ancestors and continuing on down the bloody line; their insatiable, mindless, amoral greed; their cruelty; their racist mythology; their Jim Crow laws; their feckless, self-absorbed paranoia; and their general determination to deny black Americans the most basic of rights and opportunities. Flog white people, whenever you can, with ancestral guilt for their having thrived in a nation fattened by the wage-free forced labor of millions of black men, women, and children. And spit in a white person's face that even if affirmative action were retroactively to grant to African Americans the entire monetary net worth of the American South, plus immediate tuition-free admission to any school of their choice, this would still not even begin to compensate black Americans for what is owed them.*

By this point, we all have blood trickling from our ears. Debates over affirmative action become angrier as conservative Rage Talk culture grants respectability to mean-spirited white resentments while many blacks and progressives express rage at feeling marginalized and having their arguments trivialized. The call for formal, material reparations to African Americans for slavery gains momentum as blacks see reparations being made to Holocaust survivors in Europe with no apparent white outrage or widespread moral debate. Some white views of the culpability of the poor for their own condition reach such a fever pitch that Fox pundit Bill O'Reilly can lecture the black poor in the midst of the Katrina disaster: "Connect the dots and wise up. Educate yourself, work hard, and be honest. . . . If you don't . . . the odds are that you will be desperately standing on a symbolic rooftop someday yourself. And trust me, help will not be quick in coming."[1]

But let's get one thing straight right now: this fight is not about affirmative action. Or reparations. Or welfare. Or Katrina.

This fight is about many white Americans' inability to admit, or to come to terms with, the continuing unfairness of American society and the advantages that they as whites often unknowingly take for granted. And it is about many black Americans' increasing mistrust, frustration, and rage about white hypocrisy and the prospects for remedying injustices that make the lives of blacks harder, more painful, and often shorter.

This is an argument, like much of the American quarrel over race, founded on the problem that *there are truths that belie one's own experience*. It is an argument between two broad sets of life experiences concerning racism: those of many whites to whom many of the manifestations of racism are neither personally visible nor meaningful, and those of many blacks for whom they are. It is a debate about how racially unfair a nation America actually is, and whose job it is to do something about it.

At this point, most of our news media, preoccupied as they are with shareholder returns via the profitability of pundit theatrics, are working against our having a national conversation where anyone might actually learn anything. Most of our politicians, beholden to the money and organizing power of adopted constituencies, are equally useless when it comes to this matter of overdue racial truth-telling.

So I have an idea.

Let's boil this debate down to a list of core truths that all sides, if they are to be fair, must acknowledge, and use that as a platform for solving problems that none of us, at that point, will be able to deny.

I invite you, then, on all sides of this debate, to sit down with the following short list of undeniable truths.

Undeniable Truth #1: There was a comprehensive and deliberate affirmative action program for whites decades before there was one for minorities.

What has generally not been acknowledged by historians until recently is that the New Deal and the GI Bill, which jointly created what emerged as the white middle class after World War II, did so by explicitly and deliberately designing benefits to be preferentially available to whites while erecting barriers that effectively excluded blacks. The result was classic affirmative action: the conscious selection of a particular racial group to disproportionately benefit from offered financial and educational assistance. One couldn't have asked, in fact, for a more effective affirmative action program for whites.

If this history surprises you — and it certainly

might — I commend you to a highly reviewed and impeccably documented book by Columbia University professor Ira Katznelson entitled *When Affirmative Action Was White.* In it, he explains in exhaustive detail how the crafting of legislation for the New Deal and the GI Bill was dominated, in the 1930s and 1940s, by powerful southern Democrats deeply committed to the preservation of racial segregation and white privilege. These politicians were so powerful, in fact, that President Franklin Roosevelt hesitated to resist them for fear of a filibuster that would kill his entire program. So, in the case of the New Deal, economic benefits were consciously designed to favor whites by excluding the areas of work that included most blacks: domestic and farm labor. Moreover, with local whites in charge of carrying out the law in the South, where most blacks then lived, the deck was stacked even more. Similarly, the GI Bill for housing and education, although race-neutral in theory, overwhelmingly tilted its benefits toward white men because blacks were forbidden entry to nearly all southern colleges and universities, were able to earn advanced degrees from only a few black institutions, and were commonly denied loans and mortgages and discriminated against by realtors on racial grounds. As Katznelson explains,

> At the very moment when a wide array of public policies was providing most white Americans with valuable tools to advance their social welfare — insure their old age, get good jobs, acquire economic security, build assets, and gain middle-class status — most black Americans were left behind or left out. . . . Affirmative action then was white. New national policies

enacted in the pre-civil rights, last-gasp era of Jim Crow constituted a massive transfer of quite specific privileges to white Americans. . . . To be sure, the GI Bill did create a more middle-class society, but almost exclusively for whites. Written under southern auspices, the law was deliberately designed to accommodate Jim Crow. . . . On balance, despite the assistance that black soldiers received, there was no greater instrument for widening an already huge racial gap in postwar America than the GI Bill.[2]

And so the genesis of the entire American white middle class turns out to have been a classic racially targeted affirmative action program. And the cherished idea of white suburbia having its origins in meritocracy goes up in smoke.

It is therefore a little bit late to be "debating" whether racially cognizant policies ought to play a role in shaping America.

Undeniable Truth #2: Policies of racial compensation carry a price.

The central fact to which pro-affirmative-action (and pro-reparation) blacks and progressives sometimes blind themselves is this: these measures carry a price. In the case of reparations, the price is that part of the national treasury, perhaps a significant sum, goes to the descendants of slaves as compensation for labor and suffering (the handling of the massive task of proving lineage and assigning monetary value is another conversation). In the case of affirmative action that assists blacks, the price is that some white people in some situations who would otherwise have been hired for particular jobs will not get those jobs. This needn't be because of arbitrary "quotas," a favorite bugaboo of critics. It can simply be a matter of applying standards of fairness where there once were none. If a state has a population that is one-fifth black, and whites have traditionally enjoyed a near monopoly on managerial-level government jobs in that state, mandating that 20 percent of those jobs go to blacks is not recklessly or arbitrarily applying a "quota." It is justice. At the same time, there are instances in which using quotas — hiring a temporarily heightened proportion of African Americans to bring racial balance to a roster that has been lily-white for a hundred years — is a reasonable and defensible remedy. And the resulting denial of jobs to a proportion of whites is defensible, too, as a necessary and long overdue corrective: a collective reimbursement for opportunities withheld.

But some of today's affirmative action supporters, cowed by the backpedaling in Washington and in state capitols, are afraid to stand up and meet this issue of justifiable cost and investment. They argue for affirmative action while ignoring or playing down its costs, as if no whites will lose opportunities to blacks; as if affirmative action is win-win, with no price to be paid and no moral battle to be fought and won among whites reluctant to yield ground as a make-good for whites' own historical privilege. On the key question of what America is actually willing to pay in order to redress old patterns of racism — the question at the very heart of the matter — many pro-affirmative-action partisans take a giant pass. They believe that the costs are necessary and fair, but in today's conservative-dominated environment *they are afraid to stand up in public and defend those costs.* In so doing, they pave the way for opponents to crow triumphantly, "Affirmative action does have a cost! And we Americans can't afford it!" Which, given what we now know about the history of white affirmative action, is inexcusable hypocrisy.

Would it not make a more credible case, and one better suited to honest dialogue, to acknowledge that, yes, affirmative action has a price, one that Americans have paid in the past for the benefit of whites and that the nation can and must pay now for the sake of justice? Would it not yield a better conversation for advocates of affirmative action to first acknowledge the price, and then concentrate on making the case for paying that price, rather than running away from the issue? Proponents of reparations seem more comfortable making this case, which I think is as it should be. This is the only honest way to have such a discussion.

Undeniable Truth #3: Modern affirmative action was never meant to be completely painless for white people.

What many foes of today's affirmative action steadfastly refuse to hear is this: One cannot shift the pendulum to right past wrongs of white privilege without white people needing to give something up. You simply cannot have it both ways. If you have a bigger farm than your neighbor because your great-grandfather stole some of the neighbor's land, justice involves your now giving up some land. Or some money. Or something. Moreover, given the enduring racial legacy of denied opportunity, fair-minded white Americans ought to be willing to discuss what sacrifices they are willing to make to repair the damage. For too long, the strongest moral reasoning behind modern affirmative action — the idea that it is simply the right thing to do after rampant discrimination and affirmative action favoring whites — has been excluded from the debate. It is time that this be put back on the table, time that we made the affirmative action debate a debate over what is right, not over what is least painful.

To some whites — maybe to you — this is unthinkable. How can modern American whites be called to task for wrongs committed by distant ancestors? How can a fair-minded, nonracist American white man, someone who would never imagine endorsing slavery, yield a civil service job to a black man who scored two points below him on the exam, purely as a means of offsetting an agency's historic racial discrimination? How can citizens who have never contributed directly to racial injustice be asked to help to right it?

I offer two reasons. One is a simple matter of fact and balance: for every flagrant advantage that you imagine is granted to blacks through affirmative action, there are ten granted to whites, invisibly and without fanfare, simply because they are white and therefore not subject to the same degree of scrutiny and suspicion. Absence of discrimination is, because of its very nature, a difficult thing for many whites to appreciate in their own lives. The fact is, despite whatever hardships and trials whites endure, they are passive beneficiaries of America's most aggressive affirmative action program: the one serving them. And they will never know the full extent to which this ghostly but ever-present favoritism has determined their destiny.

The other answer involves precedent. Assisting brethren, in the spirit of shared responsibility, is not a new idea. It is the foundation of health insurance, taxation, and union dues. In any civilized society — American (theoretical) social security, modern Scandinavia, and traditional Native American cultures come to mind — citizens pool resources to help one another out of jams. Moreover, the jam in which black Americans find themselves was brought about not by flood or famine, but by concerted human effort. Shouldn't Americans be willing to join a concerted effort to solve it?

For what it's worth, I would deep-six affirmative action and reparations in a heartbeat if we were to pour billions of dollars — say, something comparable to the amount spent on the Iraq War — into meaningful urban jobs and health care, thereby providing stability, income, social support, a strong tax base, funding for good schools, and a flood of qualified black graduates to sweep into American industry and academia, filling — in one fell swoop of bad-assed jet-black competency and brilliance — all the gaps in opportunity and accomplishment between the races.

In the end, we may never agree. My point is that whatever side of this debate you are on, if you expect to make progress, you are going to have to move beyond mere dogma. If you favor affirmative action or reparations, you must stand up and defend its costs in the face of its critics. If you oppose them, you must have a thoughtful answer — or admit to honest indifference — to the moral question of repairing the damage done by the lasting legacy of slavery, Jim Crow, and affirmative action for whites. Fail on either score, and you lose.

What makes the conversation intolerable for people on all sides of the issue is its tendency to get so personal. When a white person suggests that a black person wouldn't have been hired without the help of a quota, he strikes at the heart of his or her sense of worth. These are fighting words, and they elicit a fighting response. So many such attacks upon black achievement have now been made that even a general criticism of affirmative action by a white person may be taken by a black person as a direct personal assault: "Oh, so you think we're incompetent." The discussion never even gets to the more substantive issues. Maybe the warring parties would actually agree on the need for remedies. They will never know. They are too busy calling each other paranoid or racist.

And so I will conclude with five ground rules for having conversations about these issues that actually accomplish something.

Survival Suggestions

1. Talk about issues, not individuals.

Discussing how well (or badly) an individual performs his or her job should be left for formal evaluation — or to gossips. It has no place in an argument about national racial policy. Anyone can come up with convenient examples of workplace idiots or heroes. They come in all sizes and colors, and they are hired for all kinds of reasons. Anchoring your argument in "so-and-so's incompetence" will mire you in an endless battle of petty testimonials, prove nothing, and put everyone on the defensive. Save the personal insinuations for private conversations. In public debates over proposed racial policy, there is only one question: Will our communities be better off with it, or better off without it?

2. Don't start off on the defensive.

On a hot-button topic such as affirmative action or reparations, the best way to provoke a hostile response is to act as if you expect it. A preamble such as "Don't take this the wrong way . . ." is a dead giveaway to a listener that you're about to offend him. If you're that uneasy about the conversation, no prelude will help. Make a decision to wade in and take your licks, or to hold your tongue and forget about it. If you do speak, don't be terrified of disagreement. Demonstrate through your tone that you are confident of the mutual ability to argue respectfully. A display of confidence in the relationship will help the other person to relax as well — whether she agrees with your position or not.

3. Bring up the topic only when it is relevant.

Few things are more patronizing, especially to a black person, than to be asked out of the blue, "So, what do you think about reparations?" — as if being a minority makes one an automatic expert on, or a spokesman for, that minority (see chapter 7). Knowing a person very well is a different story; friendship has its own rules. Otherwise, approach these topics as you would any other controversial issue: bring it up when it seems appropriate, and in a setting conducive to honest conversation. The office hallway is a bad place. A corner table at a café is a good place.

4. If you don't want to be stereotyped, don't stereotype.

Stereotypes kill dialogues quicker than any other toxin. With regard to affirmative action, the classic white mistake

is to make sweeping judgments about minority competence. Throughout my adult life, when I have mentioned
that I graduated from Harvard, as often as not the news
has been greeted with raised eyebrows and "*You* went to
Harvard?" I have learned to come back with replies —
such as, "Yes, why do you ask?" — that stop people in
their tracks. I have no doubt that I fit Harvard's affirmative action guidelines. I also have no doubt that I belonged
there. What I find interesting, however — and what I
found true at Harvard — is that most of the white men
who seem incredulous about my achievements come from
well-off families with their own long tradition of "affirmative action" — in the form of legacy admissions to schools
their parents attended, jobs for one another's kids, and political contacts. If you want to have an intelligent conversation, you can't start it off by expressing your own stupid
presumption about the person you're talking with.

The classic conversation-killer, on the part of a black
person, is to smear a white person with a thick coat of blame
for slavery, and to presume, moreover, that all whites need to
be lectured on the subject of culpability. Whether because of
ignorance or denial, some whites do lack an understanding
of slavery's profound significance, and, further, might be
shocked to learn of the explicit affirmative action policies
that boosted whites in the twentieth century. (Many blacks,
for that matter, may also lack such an understanding.) But
casting whites as enemies, and personalizing the hostility
with a tone of "this is what you did to us," only fuels their
defensiveness. They know, whether they admit it or not,
that their ancestors did something horribly wrong. They
also know that it happened before they were born. To treat
white people as passive stewards of racism who need to be

force-fed remedies is to ignore the real conflict some of them already feel — and to shut down the potential good that inner conflict can bring, whether through confronting hard truths about affirmative action or reparations or double standards in law enforcement or some other issue. If you are going to sabotage the process, why even talk?

5. Don't assume who is "for" and who is "against."

We all know, but still need to remind ourselves, that opinions on racial policy do not strictly follow racial lines. There are blacks, as well as members of other minority groups, who question or oppose affirmative action. There are whites who champion it. The same is true for reparations and numerous other issues. If you bet on being able to anticipate "what they think," you are putting yourself in a losing position.

Identity

11

Showing Our ID:
What Is Race, Anyway?

I am "black," right?
I am the descendant of certain dark-skinned African peoples whose physical characteristics and range of cultures are generally described as "black," and I identify with that ancestry and those traditions. Correct?

And someone who is "white" has an analogously concrete relationship with his or her physical ancestry and cultural heritage. Yes? Just as someone who is, say, Asian has such a relationship with his particular physical and cultural identity. Or someone who is Eskimo. Or someone who is Arabic. Or a Pacific Islander. Right?

Well, not exactly.

There are physical characteristics of some "blacks" that I do not share. Same with culture: who is to decide how many of the infinite range of "black" cultural variations one must identify with to be demonstrably "black"? And we can ask the same questions of perceived "white" or "Asian" or "Arabic" or "Eskimo" traits. What is the standard? Can you point with authority to any given human being and identify specifically what makes her a member of her particular "race" or not?

Before you answer, consider that virtually any "black" American has an ancestry of some intermixture between "blacks" and "whites," and any "white" American has equivalent elements of "black" ancestry somewhere down the line. The intimacy of 400 years of slavery and its aftermath has made certain of that. When you factor in the simultaneous interactions with Native Americans and the flood of immigrants who have come to these shores, our tidy idea of each person's specific racial identity starts to fall apart entirely.

Then add this to the mix: all humanity originated in Africa. So we are all Africans at some essential level, with whatever further racial implications that carries.

And here's the blockbuster that blows everything out of the water: researchers now overwhelmingly agree that the very idea of race as a physical entity is scientifically meaningless. Its rules consistently break down when examined on the level of individual human beings. Scientifically speaking, race is a fiction. It does not exist. So when I write this book discussing "black" or "white" or "Arabic" or "Native American" peoples, and when you mention your "black" friend or your "white" or "Asian" coworker, what on earth are we talking about?

*   *   *

It is the question behind all the other racial questions: What is race? If it is not real, then why does it matter? And if it is real but is scientifically meaningless, then what is it? I faced this question at a public reading I once gave. A gentleman rose from the audience and asked, politely, "You predicate your book on what you call race. But geneticists have established that race is not a scientific reality. So why even talk about race? And if you think race does exist, can you explain what it is?"

The room fell quiet. This was, after all, the question of questions. Here is what I told him, which is how I believe we need to make sense of the paradoxical set of mirrors that we call race:

Race is a social construct. It is not an empirical set of physical or cultural facts. It is a set of social understandings, arrived at and continually revised in a fluid manner, about the meaning of physical traits and customs that some of us feel we have in common. In the end, it is not about the traits and customs — flat or elongated noses, kinky or straight hair, dark brown or pinkish or tan skin, oval or almond-shaped eyes, polkas or bebop, chitterlings or sushi — but about our attitudes toward them, and how we use them to define ourselves.

Name any supposedly "black" trait, for instance — a flat nose, full lips, dark skin, tight hair, a propensity for a certain cultural tradition — and I guarantee you there are Americans who possess none of these traits but who have their own reasons of ancestry and consciousness for self-identifying as "black." And so they do, and they are. Go through the entire roster of generally recognized racial identities in the world, and you will find the same thing to be true: the rules of membership always break down some-where. Some members of the racial group have certain traits but not others. Some have none of the traits that some other members have. But they are all still members. Why? Because racial membership is socially defined. It is a loose set of social decisions about how we combine appearance, ancestry, and culture in deciding who we are. This does not always involve agreement. Much of America's history of defining "whiteness" and "blackness" has been a coercive process of defining racial identity according to dominant white supremacist ideas. The old "one-drop" rule, meaning that one drop of black blood made a person officially black, was a contrived way of protecting the ostensibly superior state of whiteness from the perceived impurity of blackness. If you had one drop of blackness, your whiteness was in effect spoiled, and you were now officially black. This was, of course, absurd; one drop (whatever that means) can never pass genetic muster as a determinant of one's entire racial identity. And yet a paranoid need to defend the myth of the sanctity of whiteness gave this ridiculous idea long-standing legitimacy. There is still, today, great social pressure among both whites and blacks to define a child who has a small percentage of black ancestry as being black. Some of this, too, reflects a widespread assumption that in a society with such tilted racial values a "part-black" child may find more acceptance self-defining as "black" than as "white."

To the credit of younger generations of mixed-race Americans who refuse to accept such limiting self-definitions, this is changing. There is now a veritable mixed-race movement of organizations, Web sites, and support groups out to break free in their own chosen ways of the slavery- and Jim Crow–inspired definitions of race that dominated American culture right up through the twentieth century. As always in culturally repressive societies, mere proximity and human contact begin to save the day. The more we Americans continue to encounter one another at school, at work, and at play, the more we will befriend, intermarry, and bring down barriers among ourselves.

But whether it is a process of agreement, coercion, or rebellion against racial definitions, the point here is that race is a social phenomenon. It does not have to manifest as empirical physical fact to exist as a part of culture. It exists as an idea we have about ourselves; an idea that we pass on to our children and that we act out through our social interactions. And to the extent that it helps to shape our self-images and to drive our behavior, race is every bit as real a force as any other in the world:

- When a boss helps to shape two employees' careers by promoting one over the other for racial reasons, race is real.
- When a white person and a black person find the love of their lives together but then find their faith in each other undermined by racial tensions between their families, race is real.
- When a young white man is injured for life in a beating he receives after having blundered into a group of enraged youths in a bombed-out black neighborhood, race is real.
- On the night when African immigrant Amadou Diallo was shot forty-one times by white New York

City police officers who imagined a black man with a gun, race was real.

- When a young Arab-American woman is so traumatized at being constantly treated with suspicion in airports that she alters her lifestyle in order to stop traveling, race is real.
- When the reality TV show *Survivor* attracts a national storm of attention and fury by pitting four racial "tribes" against one another, race is real. And when another reality TV series, *Black. White.*, stirs up its own flurry by having a black family and a white family cosmetically switch races for six weeks (a stunt that goes back about fifty years to the white-authored, best-selling memoir *Black Like Me*), race is real.

Race is as real as a parent's love for a child. It exists in the ways in which we experience it and act on it. Does the world need it? Well, we certainly need the diversity. I, for one, would not want to live in a world of beige beings who all ate and did the same things. But do we need the labels? Maybe not. I think, for example, that I could live without the idea of some of us being labeled "white" and others being labeled "black." Those two terms themselves, in particular, are American shorthand created out of whole cloth. Africans were not "black" as an official category until the culture of American slavery required a way of defining them as different and inferior. And many European immigrants to America were not defined as "white" until, at a certain point in their assimilation, the cultural transition to whiteness enabled their initiation into the American middle class.[1]

But the fundamental problem is not the simple inheriting of names for ourselves. It is our having accepted the narrow, oppositional (and racist) self-definitions that came with them. I think whiteness is fine as an idea for respecting the unlimited ways in which various folks of generally European descent define their ancestries and their cultures. And I think blackness is fine as well for respecting the endless variety of ancestral and cultural self-definitions of differing peoples of generally African descent. The work we need to do now is to strip whiteness of its old mantle of superiority and normalcy, and to strip blackness of its burden of inferiority and exoticism. The dice are loaded, of course, by Western culture's traditional association of white with good and black with evil (a tendency not shared in some African cultures). That is one reason why I like "African American," although I also use "black."

But who says the white West should get to write the rules? The idea is for me to be able if I so choose to include "blackness," or any other racial quality, in my self-definitive vocabulary in a way that serves the identity I create and embrace — and for all of us, as Americans of differing but never scientifically distinct backgrounds, to be able to do the same. I want for race to be — and for all of us to understand it to be — an entity as casually and delightedly appreciated as the scent of flowers from next door or the colors of a sunset on a particular night, with all of the nonexclusivity of meaning that those pleasures imply.

Race is real. That's for sure. The trick is for us to shape the idea of race as a part of our fuller expression of who we really are.

Survival Suggestions

1. Realize that race is an idea.

Understand that what we mean when we say "I am black" or "I am white" is, "I embrace certain things about my physical ancestry and customs that connect me with other people who use this term in describing ourselves." We do not mean, "You can count on me to believe X or to behave like Y." Every racial identity is like a story containing a million different chapters, all valid and all different and often overlapping. Treat race this way, and you give it room to truthfully express itself. Treat it instead as a fixed set of physical and cultural traits, and you lock yourself and others into untrue — and often destructive or hurtful — versions of identity.

2. Realize that race is real.

Race may be an idea, but it is an idea that has real and often shattering impact as a social construct. The antebellum idea of race shored up American slavery for centuries. More modern ideas of race have led to black churches being bombed, Arab Americans being profiled and attacked, whites being accosted or viewed with hostility in certain black neighborhoods, and black men being beaten or shot by officers who looked at them and assumed the worst. Race is as real a part of culture as hunger or joy, and we ignore its history and its effects at our peril.

3. Don't let others define your identity for you.

You may feel pressure, especially if you are young, to adopt a stance toward your ancestry and cultural heritage dictated by others. Don't get me wrong: I believe it is important for young people to understand and respect their cultural traditions. But at a certain point in your growing up, you get to decide how to view them. The fact that race and culture are social constructs is precisely what gives you the power to determine their meaning for you. Your identity, including your attitude toward your racial identity, is yours and no one else's. Maybe you want to explore it. Maybe you're clear about what you want to embrace. Maybe you don't want to define yourself racially at all. It's your life and your decision.

12

You My Nigga:
Who's Naming Whom?

I t has been said of many immigrants that they became white only after arrival in America. The late Richard Pryor used to do a stand-up bit in which he described newly arrived immigrants at Ellis Island being drilled on how to properly pronounce the preferred American term for black people: "Nigger! . . . Nigger! . . . Nigger! . . . Nigger! . . ."

One could argue that whiteness was invented in America; it appeared, as a suddenly compulsory trait among the landowning classes, at roughly the same time that manacled blue-black Africans began descending ramps from ships. A subsequent procession of immigrants who were mistreated in America — Irish, Italians, Eastern Europeans — seized upon whiteness as a literal ethnic whitewashing that could usher them into the respectable American mainstream. Historian Thomas A. Guglielmo used the term "White on Arrival" to describe Italian immigrants arriving in Chicago in the early 1900s.[1] Skin color, along with the mythologies springing from it, has remained our national preoccupation ever since, taking yet another recent turn in paranoid symbology with the post-9/11 anxieties regarding Americans of Arab descent. So it is no surprise that as a nation, we have, to date, spun through at least a half-dozen names for blackness and a growing list for whiteness in the space of the past hundred years.

Okay. But what makes *black* preferable to *Negro*, and *Negro* preferable to *colored,* and *African American* preferable to all of them? Who gets to decide between *Caucasian, white,* and now, *European American*? Is there logic behind this evolution of forms of address, and can we put it to good use in an attempt to understand one another? Or, as the Paleolithic Rage Talkers like to shout, is it all nothing but linguistic political correctness?

Never, ever let anyone talk you into believing that names, in the skinfest that we call American cultural consciousness, do not matter. They do. Moreover, our long and ragged process of racial self-appellation has its own compelling logic. From the black side, beginning with *colored,* and ending (so far) with *African American,* names for Americans of African descent have grown increasingly specific in acknowledging our origins. It is no coincidence that this has been accompanied by a deepening pride in African heritage and in trans-Atlantic family lineage. For a people brought here forcibly as slaves, and labeled for centuries as being without history, the embrace of connections with our past is vital to defining who we have become.

To some, especially to whites, such meditation by blacks on the meaning of names may seem strange. Why should it make any difference? Taken by themselves, *colored* and *Negro* are fairly bland terms that, emptied of historical associations, might be arguably as good as any other. But names are more than letters and sounds. They signify much more than mere physical description. To many black people, the terms *colored* and *Negro* are mired in Jim Crow America, when segregation was accepted as law and lynchings were weekend blood sport for crowds of white families. *Colored* and *Negro* (or its purposely derogatory southern white vernacular version, *Nigra*) became, in their very sounds, sharp signifiers of flagrant racial hatred, labels chosen and uttered with malice by whites. The rise of the term *African American* represents an act of self-definition — a reclaiming of personal legacy by black people in this country. In that sense, if you are white, the choice of names for black people is not yours to make or to judge. Even if you do not understand it, respect it.

As for the mechanics of usage: for Americans of African descent, *African American* is appropriate in all situations, and is now preferred. *Black* is also generally accepted as shorthand, and is often (as in this book) used interchangeably with *African American*. (Remember, though, that *black* covers a broader category than *African American*; a black citizen of Ghana or Italy is not an African American.) Some people capitalize the first letter of *black,* believing that this constitutes a stronger statement of identity. Others, like me, believe that *black* and *white,* not being used as proper nouns (that is, not references to specific peoples or places), should not be capitalized. This is a matter of preference and, sometimes, debate. There are some African Americans who take offense at lower-case *black* but who accept it when capitalized. There are others who take offense at anything but *African American*. There are others, including a black man who rose to respectfully make his feelings known at one of my readings, who do not like the term *African American*. My experience, however, has been that most blacks will not get riled over the use of either term. I prefer *African American,* but I also consider *black* acceptable; using both, particularly when writing, can help to cut down on repetition, as when a Mexican American also uses *Chicano.*

In its period of greatest popularity (the 1960s and '70s), *Afro-American* was a significant step forward in acknowledging links to Africa. Its ongoing use in academic settings (e.g., "Afro-American Studies" departments) still lends it some legitimacy. But the phrase, to my mind, has always been a poor compromise (what is *Afro* besides a hairdo? Some vague not-quite-African past?) and has now been generally eclipsed. Better to avoid it. As for *Negro* and *colored,* both have long since fallen from favor. Avoid them entirely. Even people who grew up calling themselves *Negro* or *colored* are, with few exceptions, no longer comfortable with these terms, and anyone who came of age in the 1960s or later is almost certain to take offense. (Note, however, that "people of color" is a widely used and accepted phrase in reference to all peoples of non-European descent.) As for addressing those few who stubbornly prefer *colored* or *Negro* to anything else — you're going to have to offend somebody. Choose.

For Americans of European descent, *European American* has recently emerged as an alternative term to *white,* although it has gained nothing near the compelling popularity of *African American*. Most whites simply do not feel the need for a term that refers explicitly to Europe. Given the overwhelming manner in which those of European ancestry have dominated official American history, practically all who hear the term *white* will implicitly make the European connection. Contrast this with the experience of African Americans, who have long hungered to break the silence (and dispel the misrepresentations) shrouding their past. Among whites who feel an analogous hunger to anchor themselves in European tradition (the more zealous amateur genealogists of European family lineage come to mind, as do, in the extreme case, certain white supremacists), *European American* has a powerful appeal.

I see *European American* as a discretionary term that is interchangeable with *white* most of the time. If you are white and you feel that *European American* best describes you, use it; if it matters enough to you, make your preference known to others. It is reasonable, I think, for a person with such feelings to ask friends and acquaintances to refer to him or her as a *European American*. It is going too far, though, to expect universal preference for *European American* in the way that *African American* is preferred for blacks. As I said, with American culture having celebrated its European roots and ignored (or vilified) its African ones, black Americans have experienced a basic erosion of identity that most white Americans have not. In our nation's notion of history, Europe is central and Africa peripheral or invisible. As I have heard many blacks quip over America's lack of a designated month for white history: "Every month is White History Month."

There may be instances in which white persons of non-European ancestry (say, white immigrants from Australia or Brazil) choose a specific term (*Australian American, Brazilian American*) rather than the catchall *white*. Again, others should honor such persons' wishes; it seems to me that both the specific and general terms are appropriate, depending upon how closely a person identifies with his country of origin. If you are black, respect a white person's choice in this matter as you would expect him to respect your own.

There is often a difference between how people refer to themselves and how they expect to be referred to by others. Particularly within historically oppressed groups of Americans, such self-appellation can serve to strengthen a sense of oneness, a sense of unity, a feeling that some experience is "just between us." There are, for example, few cryptic synonyms for whiteness that are meant to be understood only by American Caucasians. There are, however, many such self-defining terms among Jews, peoples of color, and other groups whose history has made them feel outside of the mainstream. Among blacks, calling one another "brother" and "sister" is a symbolic way of saying, "We are in this together." To refer to a third party as a "brother" or a "sister" is shorthand for saying that he or she is black and therefore shares a certain understanding. Despite having been appropriated by countless synthetic hipsters of all races, it is a form of self-address that retains its potency.

Today, some progressive black leaders make it a point to refer to any person of good will as a *brother* or a *sister,* the implicit message being that justice transcends skin color. But in casual use, the terms tend to be reserved for blacks and for those few whites who are accepted as culturally "black." Other whites who fling around such terms in black company will likely find the reception chilly.

I once learned what it feels like to commit such a gaffe. I was having a conversation with a Native American woman who fliply referred to herself as a "skin," an abbreviated self-appropriation of the traditionally offensive *redskin.* The way she took the term for her own use, and the very sensation of the word *skin,* sounded so cool and fun to me that I unthinkingly opened my mouth and used *skin* to refer to myself as a person of color. I was immediately and sternly reprimanded; the term, as a derivative of *redskin,* was, she said, to be used by Native Americans only. Perhaps she expressed the feeling of most Native Americans; perhaps not. All the same, the lesson is that "just between us" speech can be closely guarded, and its rules cannot be taken for granted. If you do not know the language and its culture well, do not try to speak it.

This brings us to that thermonuclear implement of insider (and outsider) slang, *nigger.* There is a long history among black Americans of using *nigger,* both as an insult (sometimes playfully) and as a defiant display of self-contempt. I remember, as a child, trading spirited accusations of "Nigger!" along with the occasional dirt clod, with other children in the black neighborhood where my family lived until I was eight years old. Ours was the same mixed message as that of many black children who fling the word at one another today: On one level, we were appropriating a potent word for our own use in an age-old game of verbal "gotcha." Just beneath, though, we were telling ourselves, "I am a nigger. I am somewhat less than white. And I feel safer going ahead and calling myself and my friends niggers than waiting for white people to call us niggers."

To make any moral pronouncement about how people should and should not describe themselves is inherently risky. Such judgment implies an ability to read people's minds, to understand what they mean when they embrace a certain word. There is no way for anyone to assess the self-esteem of every black person who calls himself or someone else a nigger, just as it is impossible to correctly diagnose self-hatred in every gay man who playfully calls another a faggot. People juggle knives when they play with their own stereotypes. Whether they emerge lacerated or unscathed has to do with much more than their vocabulary. I know some African Americans who decry any use of *nigger* by black people — but who then turn around and display such classic symptoms of self-hatred as referring to straight, Caucasian-like hair as "good hair." I also know supremely confident, racially proud African Americans who occasionally kid one another in private with the term *nigger*.

I once, as a guest on a midwestern radio talk show with a largely white audience, nearly gave the white host a heart attack by uttering the word *nigger* on the air as a way of introducing my thoughts about the word itself. I will never forget the look of terror on his face; the word was such a taboo that it was considered impermissible to say it even when having a discussion about it. There are some good reasons for this. *Nigger,* a misspelled derivation of *niger,* the Latin word for "black," has as evil and bloody a history as any word in the English language. It is hard for me to imagine any reasoned justification for us blacks to use the word in the traditional way, as a real or playful insult. I have yet to hear anyone make a cogent argument in its defense. I believe that children should be told of the epithet's wicked history, and taught not to use it. But those (such as myself) who disapprove of the word must also beware of our own tendency to stereotype all blacks who use it. Whether we like it or not, playful use of *nigger* can, like telling "black" jokes (which I'll discuss later), fall into the category of things that self-respecting black adults feel they oughtn't do but sometimes do anyway. The only way to knowledgeably judge a person is to know him.

In the 1980s, another black appropriation of *nigger* began to appear as a virtual mantra in violent gangsta rap: *nigga*. For such 1980s rappers as N.W.A. (Niggaz With Attitude) and the early Ice-T, being a nigga meant being the ultimate outlaw, being an armed desperado with the power to destroy yourself before white society could do the job. It meant invulnerability through suicide. It proved to be an irresistible image, both for young would-be black gangstas who wished for power through guns and money, and for alienated white suburban kids who sought safe rebellion through their stereos. It also proved colossally profitable for the recording industry, which, despite concessions to pressure from political and religious groups, has to this day continued to sell this image of the young black male identity in a variety of forms. A few months ago in a music store, I saw a white child, perhaps ten years old, point eagerly to a photograph of a barechested, muscled, scowling black hip-hop artist and say with hushed glee to his sister, "I heard he's been shot *fifty times!*"

The 1980s' and early '90s' defiant use of *nigga* as self-reference by young black people captured, more than any other act, the desperate dilemma of black identity: self-hatred coupled with a stubborn resolve for self-determination. To proclaim oneself a nigga was to declare to the disapproving mainstream, "You can't fire me. I quit." Hence the immediate popularity of the word among poor black youth who carried, at the same time, a burning resentment of white society. To growl that one was a "nigga" was a seductive gesture of self-caricature — and one that may have felt bitterly empowering. In some ways it was as inherently destructive as the white baying of "coon," "jungle bunny," "moolie," and all the rest. But it was also an assertive way of getting in the face of a society in which nervous suburbanites crossed the street to avoid them and locked their car doors against them. For many young black males, angry self-sacrifice felt, and still feels, like one of their few remaining paths to personal power.

Then something else happened. Use of *nigga* mellowed to also become a term of shared endearment, as in a loyal friend's being "my nigga." While we adults clucked at black youngsters' lack of historical understanding in choosing to dress up this oppressive word for collegial use, they went right ahead and built *nigga* into the vernacular of hip-hop and youth culture in general. What happened next could have been predicted: white youths, homing in on black pop culture as they have since the days before Elvis, flocked to hip-hop and took up "nigga" as a cause célèbre. You can now visit a virtually all-white suburban high school and hear white kids telling each other "You my nigga" and "You so ghetto."

Do I like the word? No. Will I ever feel comfortable using it? Probably not. But I am not prepared to pronounce all of the black young people who now use *nigga* this breezily as being guilty of self-hatred. Nor do I believe for a moment that the white students who now run around parroting "nigga" expressions dislike black people. They might not *know* any or many black people, but it is pretty clear that they feel (as white kids have for a century now) that blackness is the coolest thing on the planet. Or, at least, the version of blackness that makes its way to them.

Here is an anecdote that pretty well sums up the "nigga" saga as a cultural and political work in progress: Recently at a suburban Maryland high school, the yearbook was mysteriously altered just before press time so that the photo caption of a mixed-race student was changed to include "nigga." The yearbook was distributed before the deed was discovered. All hell broke loose. The yearbook was recalled, which students and parents protested. The news media grabbed the story. Civil rights advocates called for an investigation. It turned out, however, that the change had been made as a prank by a white buddy of the mixed-race student, that "nigga" had been a longtime part of their shared vocabulary, and that the two of them found the entire public "nigga" controversy to be hilarious.

What is the moral of the story? Ask me in another five years. What we know now is that black youth, as before, are taking language in new directions, and white youth, as before, are following, and that the mainstream, as always, is about three steps behind. In a society in which power, stature, choice, and so much else are skewed by race, the perils of black self-hatred and white stereotyping (and exploiting) of blackness are always present. But so is the endless process of evolution toward new levels of culture.

Meanwhile, in the plodding adult mainstream, certain basic rules apply. If you are white, use of *nigger* is completely off-limits, unless you happen to be one of the few whites so deeply assimilated into black life that it is not an issue. If you have to ask yourself whether using *nigger* is okay, it is not. An African American who uses *nigger* is playing with fire, but it is his own property — his identity — that he places at risk. A white American who cries "nigger" is lighting a blaze in someone else's house, and will likely be treated as an arsonist.

There are as many ugly synonyms for whiteness as there are for blackness, and you have probably heard them all: *honky, cracker ofay, snow girl, punk,* and so on. The same principles of decorum and self-respect apply here as well. One significant difference, though, is that through the sheer weight of white racism in our society, antiblack epithets carry much more destructive firepower than antiwhite ones. Or, put another way, a much higher proportion of blacks call themselves niggers than whites call themselves honkies. The effect is that while the collective black psyche is strafed by artillery fire, the white psyche fends off an occasional BB pellet.

As I've said, this imbalance holds true for all racist exchanges between blacks and whites in America. It does not, however, change the essential rules of decent human conduct: Calling people bad names is wrong. Don't do it. And if you call yourself bad names, ask yourself why.

Survival Suggestions

1. Understand that people have the right to name themselves.

Even if you can't see the meaning of *African American* or *European American,* respect someone's right to use it as a self-appellation.

2. Understand that the term *African American* is driven by particularly powerful needs.

African American answers a desire among many blacks to reconnect with a heritage from which they were forcibly estranged by slavery, racism, and a European-centered view of history. The same dynamic does not hold true for most white Americans. It is fair, then, to expect a greater sense of urgency, and greater prevalence of use, with *African American* than with terms American whites might use in relation to their cultural ancestry.

3. Understand that when you play with other people's language, you play with fire.

Language changes. *Nigga* is no longer the same word as *nigger*. And yet, these words remain loaded with four hundred years' worth of brutal history, and racial resentments continue about who owns them and what they mean. Whether you're black or not, you're free to say what you like in what you think is a well-meaning way. But understand what you're dealing with — and what you might come up against as a result of your choice of language.

4. If you know it's an insult, don't use it. Ever.

If you're white, forget about ever calling a black person a "nigger." If you're black, forget about ever calling a white person an "ofay" or a "snow girl" or a "honky." The exceptions are: (1) If you're looking to get punched or shot, and (2) If you know the person so intimately that this rule doesn't apply, in which case you don't need to be reading this.

13

Congratulations! You're Ethnic!

My nearest dictionary at hand defines ethnic as: "1. Heathen; pagan; pertaining to nations or groups neither Christian nor Jewish. 2. Designating or of any of the basic divisions or groups of mankind, as distinguished by customs, characteristics, language, etc."

Right off, there's a conflict: by old-fashioned standards of white ethnocentrism (as in the first definition above), only swarthy non–Western Europeans — that majority of the world's population seen as exotic "others" — rate the label of ethnic. But by modern standards (as in the second definition), everybody is ethnic: you, me, Paris Hilton. This sows terrible confusion among crowds at Disney World. What constitutes cultural normalcy? Do we stick with the fabled

ethnic folklore of European conquest, with Yul Brynner as
the wild-eyed King of Siam and Deborah Kerr as the civi-
lized soul who tames him? Or do we embrace the more re-
cent definitions in our dictionaries, updated with the help
of immigration and sit-ins?

Crossed signals fly everywhere. Hip-hop star and actress
Queen Latifah has brought out a new line of makeup for
women of color to the national retail market. In many
stores, you will find smiling black faces pictured among
the greeting cards. Meanwhile, all of the black hair products are often still to be found crammed beneath a sign
marked "Ethnic," while presumably nonethnic hair goo
for Caucasians goes by such placidly universal shelf sig-
nage as "shampoos" and "dyes." Our schools preach a
singsong "diversity" gospel ("we're all weird and we're all
normal") almost to the point of genuflection. Yet, in a
popular guide to university scholarships, I stumbled across
a fund for minority students with the stated purpose of
providing "financial assistance to students of ethnic origin." As opposed, I guess, to students of nonethnic origin.
And when American academics refer to "ethnic" or "cultural" studies, they generally mean brown- or red- or yel-
low-bannered encampments, not those astonishingly
European-focused camps demurely labeled "History" or
"Languages."

   You could call all of this just more soul-on-your-
sleeve multicultural carping. After all, why should we care
what things are labeled as long as we can find them in supermarkets and in classrooms?

   I'll tell you why. Because when you buy into the peripheral "ethnicity" of nonwhites, and the central "non-

ethnicity" of whites, whether with supermarket products or college curricula, you buy into a massive ethnocentric lie. Like astronomers before Galileo, you entertain a false idea of what (or who) resides at the center of all things. Like anyone with a bad map, sooner or later — in these increasingly nonwhite environs — you are going to not know where you are.

Many Americans — of all races — suffer from a widespread delusion that "ethnicity" is a characteristic limited to people of color, an odd sort of cultural texturing that whites and their traditions are presumed to lack. Looked at this way, ethnicity becomes a subtle but indelible scarlet letter of nonwhiteness, a marker dye separating that which is familiar from that which is, well, different. It becomes a way of placing white culture, in particular, in a category apart from all others, a way of exempting whiteness from any sense of cultural relativism, and of therefore keeping white culture firmly at the center of approved American reality — while the perceived "ethnic" cultures whirl about as orbiting social satellites. By this definition, the sound of Hispanic salsa music blaring from an apartment window and the wafting aroma of a black chicken-and-ribs restaurant are both ethnic, while the munching of a tuna sandwich on white bread by a white Anglo-Saxon man in green pants is, hysterically enough, normal. My point is that, increasingly, we all are coming to recognize that white Americans are ethnic, too.

I mean, how much more ethnic can you get than hair that, of all things, falls limply in any direction instead of kinkily holding its own? What could be more ethnic a trait than sunburn? Or than wearing shorts in winter? Or — here's a bizarre one for you — than insisting that music be written down and performed by rote (rather than composed in spontaneous reverie), in order to qualify as a serious effort of the human heart and intellect? For that matter, how much more strange could any culture be than the technology-intoxicated, increasingly dispirited society in which we now live? How can anyone, anywhere, make any pretenses to nonethnicity or cultural inertness?

Getting suckered into believing the nutty idea of cultural centrality will damage people more than they know. To give just one example, obstinate white huddling around inherited European forms is why, tragically, America ranks somewhere near last in the world — certainly well behind Japan and all of Europe — in appreciating the significance of jazz. And by jazz I do not mean Tommy Dorsey or Kenny G. I mean men and women, mostly but not exclusively African American, schooled in the merciless crucible of public musical improvisation, in which gemlike technical mastery is expected and instant fluency in all keys of one's soul is demanded. Every night. In front of strangers.

You'll notice that I'm not talking about whether or not Americans like jazz. I'm talking about whether or not they recognize its stature, in the way that, say, a woman who has never once listened to Beethoven will reflexively utter his name when her third-grade son asks her to name a "great" musician for his school assignment. Her confidence that Beethoven is central to music has nothing to do with liking or even knowing his art. His importance is one of a thousand cultural facts that she memorized at an early age. She hasn't the least bit of feeling for his music's heart-bursting intensity. But she knows that he matters. A lot.

In the same way, you can dislike or even hate jazz and still give it its due as one of the most significant forms of artistic expression of the past century. It is easily the harmonic and rhythmic equal (if not better) of any of the world's most sophisticated musical forms, including those by the more difficult European composers. And heart? Listen to Charlie "Bird" Parker, blowing those genius wormtrains of Swiss-synchronized chords at warp speed, each chosen, impossibly, with angelically lyrical foreknowledge. There is Miles Davis, creating, literally, his own language of tight-throated, galaxy-spaced tonal travel. There is Billie Holiday, making of the human voice a newly flared horn. There is John Coltrane, reincarnating Western scales and Eastern modes in hurricane prayer spasms that reduced the thronged faithful in New York basement nightclubs to howls and shivers.

But, as I said, you might hate jazz. There are plenty of people in Tokyo and in Paris who do. Even a French or Japanese jazz hater, though, is far likelier than an American to acknowledge the music's importance, its place in the world of modern serious music. Ask any jazz musician how he is received in Europe, Asia, or Africa as compared with America, and you will hear how Americans undervalue jazz. Joachim Berendt, to name one scholar among scads of them, calls jazz "America's most autonomous and important contribution to world culture." He was German. (His much-reprinted *Jazz Book,* by the way, is a must-read on black American music, as is Amiri Baraka's *Blues People.*) The first published study of jazz by a white person came from a Swiss conductor, Ernest Ansermet, in 1919. The first book on jazz was written by a Belgian, Robert Goffin, in 1929. The first jazz magazine was edited by a Frenchman, Hugues Panassié, beginning in the late 1920s. They all knew that this American music had changed the world.

Americans should know this, too. In the same way that even those of us only slightly familiar with music are willing to grant the greatness of classical music, we should know the equally monumental global stature of jazz. We could enlarge our pantheon of officially sanctioned and supported mainstream creative heroes — as opposed to the marginal "great hip genius" stature generally reserved for jazz immortals — to include Louis as well as Ludwig, Miles as well as Mozart. The same can be said about the genius of hip-hop, already emerging as the next great American art form with its slant rhymes and its whirling tongue patterns and its synapse-blowing in-the-moment complexities. Were it not for American white ethnocentric inertia, more of us might know the global artistic weight of black American art forms such as jazz and hip-hop. But many of us are not listening. In the supermarket of our national culture, black musics, whatever their artistic intensity, are relegated to the "ethnic" aisle. And our dominant idea of shampoo is the culturally "normal" kind — an aisle away.

Let me be clear: there are marginalized musical forms in America that are not black, or at least not expressly so. Moreover, some marginalization — say, not being appreciated by the young — is common to practically all classic art forms.

But no American art form, in any field, has been as venerated worldwide — as established and canonized — as jazz, in particular. It is this very global veneration that makes its diminished stature in America — its image as more entertainment than as art — so striking. It is a unique predicament that is hard to explain on any other basis than cultural bias. Having been pedigreed by so many scholars and musicians over the past century as being at the very heart of American life, jazz provides a classic example of the power of white American denial.

What you and I must realize is simply that we are all, every one of us, as gratingly ethnic in our manners and habits as my fattest and loudest and brassiest relative; we are all as improbable and as inexplicable as the Zen poet sheep rancher I met in Wyoming; we are all as odd as gefilte fish or white bread or American cheese or roasted tapir; we are as enigmatic as voodoo and sacrificed chickens and acupressure and the sweat-lodge ceremony.

Being ethnic means being alive. Each of us on this planet, no matter how serene our notion of normalcy, is as bizarre and unbelievable an ethnic creation as the world has ever seen. And we are surrounded by billions of people who know it. Our national game of bland non-ness, of objective centrality, is lost; give it up. As you go through whatever social motions you might find familiar — applying suntan lotion, teaching about the Pilgrims, spreading blue cheese on expensive crackers, doing an Elvis imitation, combing your hair — remind yourself: this is ethnic. Begin to consider your characteristics, and your customs, as being no less strange than those of, say, your immigrant neighbors who cook that funny-smelling food. Which is to say, understand that those neighbors view you the same way.

While you're at it, stop buying into the "ethnic" labeling in supermarkets. In fact, if you own a store, change your signs. If you need a sign highlighting black hair products, what's wrong with "African American"? Okay, maybe it's a hassle referring to groups by name. But are you unwilling to expend a few extra minutes, or a few extra cents, to do the right thing for your customers? And if you want to save trouble and expense, shelve all of the items together as "hair products."

For a sharpened sense of what it means to share the world, pick up a copy of *The Dictionary of Global Culture* by Kwame Anthony Appiah and Henry Louis Gates Jr. From Arabic literature to traditional Japanese clothing, from American presidents to Lebanese poets, it's an alphabetically ordered reminder of the vastness of everything we call culture.

Here's wishing that you will never have to feel nonethnic again.

Survival Suggestions

1. Think about the fact that you are ethnic.

As an experiment, if you have not had the experience of thinking of yourself and your habits as "ethnic," do so. Imagine the utter strangeness of your physical features, your diet, and the music you like from the point of view of someone whose way of being is entirely alien to yours. It's a good way of sharpening your enjoyment of what makes you, and others, different.

2. Actively resist others' ethnocentrism.

In your personal life and at work, resist the subtle ways in which others may present their ethnic realities as being central or "normal." Sometimes this might seem trivial — say, a friend or coworker describing certain peoples or cuisines or musics as "ethnic" — but its implications are huge. People who view their ethnic experiences as being the standard for normalcy need to be reminded, for the sake of the collective good, that they are not.

3. Don't tolerate "Ethnic" signs in stores.

When you see particular types of goods, such as black hair products or Asian foods, lumped under the "ethnic" label while other products are not, let the store manager know that you do not appreciate the underlying assumption. Suggest instead that they be labeled as simply "African American" or "Asian" or whatever, or, in cases where there is no practical reason to separate them, that they be treated as "normal" and shelved with similar items of other ethnicities. Again, this may seem a minor thing. But it is not. It gets to the heart of how Americans view themselves and one another.

14

Elvis to Eminem: Black Music and the Fight over Who Owns Culture

[Elvis] was the first person in America to get a hysterical white mob to approach a black phenomenon without violating the Bill of Rights.

— Mark Crispin Miller

Eminem is as close as a [white] kid can come to being black, at least in anger and attitude. And white kids, many of them, want to be black.

— Rob Morse, *San Francisco Chronicle*

I want to tell you an old, old story:

Once upon a time there was a group of lighter people who forced a group of darker people to live with them and work for them for free. Once the brutal free-work thing was ended, the darker people still weren't entirely liberated, but made gradual progress over many years struggling against often vicious subjugation and toward fair treatment. Meanwhile, the darker people had brought with them all kinds of sophisticated customs, some of them musical, which the lighter people at first banned (so the darker people would make better slaves) but also liked. The darker people managed to hold on to some of these musical customs, first in secret during slavery and then openly afterward. They also blended them with the lighter people's musical customs, creating exciting kinds of music that nobody had ever heard before. The lighter people loved this, even though they didn't always like the darker people themselves so much. The lighter people felt great listening and sometimes dancing to these new musics created by the darker peoples, but many of them also felt a little funny about it because they had taught themselves to view the darker peoples as primitive and inferior. So a lot of the "darker" music was filtered for the lighter people by bands of lighter musicians who learned to play easy, watered-down versions of the original darker styles.

But there were also lighter musicians who wanted to play the true darker music. And there were also many lighter listeners, especially young people, who hungered to hear and dance to the real darker music. For these young lighter people, hearing the real thing — at darker nightclubs and on recordings called "race records" aimed at darker audiences — became a rebellious craving. This caused trouble in a society that was still trying to keep the lighter and darker peoples apart.

Then something happened: Some lighter singers and musicians learned to perform the darker music so well that their recordings thrilled the young lighter fans. For the companies that sold music, it was the perfect arrangement: They could profit from the excitement of the darker music while sidestepping society's discomfort with race-mixing. Moreover, the companies found that many lighter fans felt even more drawn to the music once they saw it being performed by lighter musicians; it helped fans feel that this darker music was now "their" music as well. Under the banner of lighter stars, darker music sold to lighter audiences like never before. It was a gold mine.

But not for everybody. Many darker musicians saw their styles mimicked and their careers (and earnings) eclipsed by young lighter copycats. Some darker people resented, either privately or vocally, the exploitation of darker music for the gain of the careers and companies of lighter people. Lighter musicians who "made it" playing darker-styled music had to either show their "propers" of respect for their darker forbears or suffer disrespect among the darker musicians whom they themselves revered. Some lighter superstars were hounded by the guilt they felt.

Years have passed. Darker people have continued to lead the way with popular music trends; lighter musicians and fans have followed. Fans and musicians have intermingled more and more, to the point where the old idea of forbidden racial "mixing" around music now feels archaic. But beneath the shared space, familiar questions lurk: Why do lighter fans like darker music best when it is brought to them by lighter performers? Why, as a result, do the lighter interpreters of dark music become bigger stars and make more money than the darker ones who are arguably closer to the music's source? And, in the end, whose music is it?

In a sense, those questions themselves are the story.

We have today, I would say, two main musical parables for these questions of cultural ownership. One is named Elvis. The other, as if in alliterative partnership, is named Eminem.

First to Elvis, who has definitely *not* left the building.

Before the chins, before the shovel-sized belt buckles and the carpeted Graceland ceilings, Elvis Aron Presley was a quiet, skinny white kid from Tupelo, Mississippi, with bad acne and a deep love of music: rhythm and blues, hymnal, hillbilly.

These days, of course, Elvis is popularly mocked and mourned as a sideburned patron saint of kitsch and mortal excess, respectively; enthroned as "The King" by lifelong fans for whom hipness calcified somewhere between Pat Boone and James Brown; reviled by many as a strutting symbol of white exploitation of black music. He may be subject to more eye-rolling among blacks than anyone this side of Al Jolson.

There can be no doubt that Elvis consciously built his hit persona upon black music. As Peter Guralnick made clear in the first volume of his exhaustive Elvis biography, *Last Train to Memphis,* black R&B lay at the heart of his recording career. Sun Records founder Sam Phillips, the first to record Elvis, made no bones about it: "[Black] records appealed to white youngsters just as Uncle Silas

[Payne's] songs and stories used to appeal to me. . . . But there was something in many of those youngsters that resisted buying this music. . . . They liked the music, but they weren't sure whether they ought to like it or not. So I got to thinking how many records you could sell if you could find white performers who could play and sing in this same exciting, alive way."[1]

What Phillips recognized as the breakthrough in Elvis's early studio sessions came when, after fruitless hours of doodling with ballads, Elvis broke spontaneously into a rendition of black R&B artist Arthur "Big Boy" Crudup's "That's All Right (Mama)." Phillips sat up straight. Tape rolled. The rest is history: Elvis's string of five consecutive hits for Sun in 1954 and 1955, including Wynonie Harris's "Good Rockin' Tonight" and Little Junior Parker and The Blue Flames' "Mystery Train." All were either covers of R&B tunes or country songs sung in R&B style.

That is why, when his voice was first launched over the airwaves throughout the unsuspecting American South, Elvis Aron Presley sounded black. Very black. So black, in fact, that his first radio interviewer, in Memphis, made it a point to have Elvis mention to listeners that he had attended (segregated) Humes High School. As the interviewer later explained to a writer, "I wanted to get that out, because a lot of people listening had thought he was colored."[2]

In *Boxed In: The Culture of TV,* Mark Crispin Miller goes even further: "Elvis' appropriation of blackness was not restricted to his music. . . . Like Brando, he did not look entirely white (a statement that might have annoyed him), but seemed a curious amalgam of the races: with his full lips, broad nose, and jet-black hair (dyed), he was a new kind of idol, looking ahead to such Sixties celebrities as Mick Jagger and Malcolm McDowell."[3]

But even as he raided the R&B catalog and moved in the shadow of blackness, Elvis made astonishing and enduring entries of his own in the lexicon as a singer, a performer, and a musical superhero: His machine-gun leg movement, cranking epileptically in the billowing fabric behind his knife-edged pant crease as if he were being rhythmically peeled to the bone. His patented pelvis, not just suggestively undulating but childishly herky-jerky, grinding out a message of salvation for teenage refugees from the white puritanical tradition. His voice, poised between stab and sob. And that perfectly ugly sneer, its weepy threat of babylike violence complemented by his downturned lips and eyes. This was no mere lip-synching of "race records." This was all Elvis, the kind of thing you might well expect from a kid who, as Elvis's adolescent friends seem to unanimously recall, was always kind of strange.

So why pick on Elvis as America's illicit spice trader? Because he provides such an obvious racial meeting place. His famed pelvis is literally the modern pivot point, the commercial bone-and-socket at which our jangling black and white limbs are connected. Elvis is where Johnnie Ray meets Madonna, and where Bob Dylan meets Fats Domino. Elvis is where a white girl in Cleveland dances, metaphorically, with a black boy in Jim Crow Alabama. Elvis is where miscegenation in American music officially went big-time. Deny Elvis, and you deny the very fact of black and white American dancers being joined at the hip.

Elvis — the young Elvis, the thin Elvis — went into the studio and got crazy. He didn't map out a scheme to go crazy; he just went crazy, honky-tonk crazy, with the music he had always loved, and on the air and in the record stores a certain dark craziness suddenly became permissible and accessible for hordes of young white listeners. And then Elvis went to Hollywood. And the Chords and Big Joe Turner and Wynonie Harris and La-Vern Baker and Little Richard and the scores of other black pioneers of the dark craziness, who saw their own songs rerecorded as smash hits by white artists, were left behind (often with no copyright protection) to make chump change. It's not pretty. But it's history.

All this made up the man who came gyrating across the bridge to the white territories, not just a black-sounding singer who (hot damn!) turned out to be a white fella, but one who also opened a whole new theater of possibilities: in which hillbilly twang had a back beat and an uptown attitude; in which being mean-assed was cool; in which white girls were allowed to scream; in which sex among white teenagers at last found expression; in which sneering violence became musical eroticism; in which whites could dance with blacks without actually having to cross the tracks. Look out across any ocean-sized arena today, in which thousands of white kids roar at costumed performers ripping through amplified variations on the blues, and you can pretty well say, "Elvis was here."

Now flash forward forty years to hip-hop and a white kid from Detroit named Marshall Mathers who would later go by the name of Eminem. (Get the phonetic reference to the "M's" in his name?)

Like R&B in the 1950s, hip-hop — called "rap" in its earlier incarnations in the 1980s — had by the 1990s become the dominant musical force for American youth of all races. With its bone-shredding beats, its insatiable inclusion of audio elements from rhythmic LP scratching to music sampling to synthesized sounds, and its recklessly creative rhyming and vocal percussiveness, hip-hop left all other pop genres in the dust for raw excitement and imaginative surprise. It had its origins in the 1970s and '80s in black communities as a rebellious music made by kids with no money using available sounds and materials, and its roots extend back to the black political percussive poetry of the New York–based ensemble the Last Poets in the 1960s. By the mid-1990s the dominance of hip-hop was absolute; as I write today, early in the twenty-first century, it has long since been the top-selling music genre in America.

The hip-hop pantheon includes such artists as Grandmaster Flash and the Furious Five, whose 1970s "The Message" was arguably the first true rap record; "gangsta" crew N.W.A. (Niggaz With Attitude), who in the 1980s helped to forge the venerable and marketable image of the ruthless and profane black rapper; Public Enemy, an explicitly political group led by rappers Chuck D and Flavor Flav; Tupac Shakur, a legendary hip-hop leader who died a violent death as he tried to negotiate the territory of anger and political constructivism; Snoop Dogg, who gradually made the turn from self-styled gangsta to political activist and actor; Queen Latifah, who more than any other hip-hop artist has combated the genre's notorious misogyny with strong-female and politically constructive messages (and who now also appears in films and has her own line of cosmetics for women of color); and many others.

The largest single market for hip-hop, by a significant margin, is young whites, who, like their predecessors in the decades before them, embrace black music as the global standard for hipness. And, as with Elvis and R&B, the figure who has emerged to carry hip-hop's popularity into previously uncharted territory is white: Eminem.

The Elvis analogy is not a complete fit, however. While Eminem's unprecedented cross-racial success affirms the long-standing preference of white audiences for white standard-bearers of black music (see the early Rolling Stones, Led Zeppelin, Eric Clapton, Johnny Winter, the Allman Brothers, ZZ Top, the Black Crowes, and so on), he has always made clear his respectful awareness of being a practitioner of a black musical form. And, unlike such white show horses as the vanished and unlamented Vanilla Ice, Eminem is more than a mere consultant-crafted amalgam of faux authenticity. He is a talented performer in a black genre who happens to be white, and his preoccupation seems to be much more with the music and his message than with his credentials. I should mention here, too, that the precedent for a white artist's showing such respect for his adopted cultural milieu was set much earlier by Clapton and the Allman Brothers, among others, who always explicitly told their audiences about the black authors of the blues classics they played. (Not so with Led Zeppelin, which has been a grievance among musicians for years.)

Part of this stance on Eminem's part may be due to his having been discovered by superstar black rapper and producer Dr. Dre, who produced Eminem's first albums and was instrumental in making him a star. His 1999 debut album, *The Slim Shady LP,* went triple platinum by the end of that year, and his next, *The Marshall Mathers LP,* generally regarded by critics and fans as his best, sold millions. Subsequent albums, including *The Eminem Show* and a greatest-hits collection entitled *Curtain Call*, were not as universally praised. He has been justifiably disparaged for misogyny and homophobia in his lyrics, and in this regard he embraces the worst in hip-hop: a maliciously sensationalist brand of heterosexist adolescent male bravado. But Eminem's undeniable talents — for crafting a rhyme, pacing and dramatizing a story, and shifting rhythms and styles without losing the beat — are broadly respected within the hip-hop world, and his fans are legion and often fanatical. Part of what distinguishes him from run-of-the-mill nastyboy ranters is his lyrical plumbing of issues within his life, which has been troubled, beginning with his father's abandoning the family when Marshall was two years old and continuing with family drug issues, conflicts with his mother, a tempestuous saga of marriage-divorce-remarriageredivorce with his sometime wife, and legal battles. He is about story as well as style. He also starred in a film, *8 Mile*, about an aspiring white rapper who beats the odds, for which he won an Oscar.

And so, once again, we have a talented white performer moving to the commercial forefront of a black art form. This, I think, is more of an issue for us in the larger society than for the artists themselves. Hip-hop artists, like jazz musicians, appear to be a pretty meritocratic crew; if you've got the goods and you're down with the life, you're in, and although there can be spectacular ego clashes over very stupid things, raw ability seems to be honored among artists as a basic coin of the realm. Moreover, Eminem was discovered and promoted by a black producer who saw his talent and, rightly, believed in it. Why *shouldn't* a white performer succeed in a black art form? Should we forbid the terrific young (white) jazz tenor saxophonist Eric Alexander his well-deserved success? Should we negate the long and distinguished jazz careers of the great (and white) bassist Charlie Haden, and the innovative (and white) pianist Bill Evans, and the brilliant (and white) alto saxophonist Phil Woods?

Deep down in the works, there is a certain amount of cultural synthesis at work here alongside the appropriation, as Carl Hancock Rux explains in the conclusion of his essay on Eminem in a collection edited by Greg Tate entitled *Everything but the Burden*:

> The old White Negro may have worn cork and afro wigs, soaked up Harlem culture and delivered the talented tenth to the mainstream, given race music a haircut, tuxedo jacket, and orchestra, may have learned to shake their narrow white hips in the manner of the Negro, thereby creating just enough controversy to gain movie star status, and may have heroicized Negro jazz musicians in their literature, proudly proclaiming to have actually shared a joint or some smack with one or two Negroes at the height of a Bohemian subculture's tendency toward race mixing — but the new White Negro has not arrived at black culture . . . he was born into it — and there is a difference.[4]

The problem, of course, is that Eminem's success takes place within a setting in which the accountants who run the music industry have traditionally and consistently made "Elvis" decisions to promote white artists playing black-inspired music who become heroes to huge numbers of music-buying whites. The list of great black artists who, although successful, never got their full due in the music industry is long, and includes some immortals: Muddy

Waters, B. B. King, Chuck Berry, Ray Charles. And the underlying question, from the point of view of many blacks, has always been: Hey, who owns this music of ours, anyway? How come we start it, and then the white mainstream claims it and takes it to the bank?

The heart of the problem, to put it bluntly, is that American whites seem to prefer, or at least to better accept on a commercial level, black music when it comes to them via white performers. There is an implicit collective egocentrism, or maybe denial, here that is troubling. It is as if many white listeners, knowing as they do the dominant historical role of black artistry in having formed the music they like, require the ethnic reassurance of hearing such music rendered ably and pleasingly by their "own" people.

This, along with decades of stories about unpaid royalties to black icons, is why so many blacks roll their eyes at the mention of Elvis, and why the success of even the widely respected Eminem can trigger smirks.

Do blacks need to separate the ethical wheat from the chaff and give deserving white artists their meritocratic due? Absolutely.

But whites, for their part, need to better understand the plantation-like racial habits of the American pop music business. And they need to ask themselves why they, as fans, needed the Rolling Stones to bring them Muddy Waters, and why they needed Elvis to bring them the longed-for release of black R&B.

Therein lies the path to bona fide cultural ownership.

Survival Suggestions

1. If you are white, understand that you are being racially pandered to.

There has been a working assumption for decades in the American music industry that in order for black music to "cross over" or make it big, it needs to be brought to white audiences by white artists. If your musical taste makes you part of this pattern, ask yourself: Why?

2. Don't blame Elvis or Eminem. Blame the system that has stacked the deck.

If you resent the racial assumptions underlying how pop music is accepted, it is better to put your energy into addressing the system than stigmatizing individual artists. Elvis was talented. So is Eminem. So are many other white artists who come out of the black musical tradition. You have the right to resent them if you like. But why not aim your strongest criticism at the corporate music industry — in writing, and with your buying habits? Support smaller media, particularly online music sources, that give a broader range of musicians a shot at fame.

3. Speak up about it.

However you feel about this, make your feelings known about these issues when you talk music with other people. This is a conversation that needs to happen.

15

Hey, Yo: What Color Do You Speak?

Take this quiz:

1. A thirtyish black male customer wearing khakis and a button-down shirt approaches the counter in a convenience store. The cashier is white. How is he likely to address the black customer, about whom he knows nothing?

    __ "Yo, help you, bro?"
    __ "May I help you?"

2. A female black attorney takes a cold call from a potential client, who is white. She so impresses the client that he wants to come in and meet with her right away. At the appointed time, the client walks

into the attorney's office and sees that she is black. How is he likely to react?

__ Display his shock

__ Hide his shock

__ Consider her race unworthy of note

3. Young people speak "black English" because:

__ Schools can barely stay afloat, let alone offer instruction in elocution

__ Their families and friends speak it

__ They think standard English is for bookish punks

__ They are white, suburban, and trying to be cool

The correct answers? Well, for better or for worse, all of the above are "correct" in the sense that they reflect what actually happens, or they explain things that you and I face every day. And they tell us something essential: speech is a high-stakes ethnic code, a set of clues we use to make instant decisions about strangers.

We screen one another's language as if we are soldiers on a scouting mission. You see a youngish black man in a store? You make him, in your mind's eye, walk the walk and talk the talk, even if he is a medical student from Shaker Heights. You talk to someone on the phone who speaks standard English? She's white. It's automatic. Her being black does not even appear on the radar screen of possibilities; mastering the language of mainstream achievement is a white thing, right? Black kids whose schools have no textbooks learn that lesson early.

Language is loaded. Speaking mainstream English as I do, I am regularly mistaken for white on the telephone — a wild contrast to the way in which I am commonly taken for a yo in person. In my days as a newspaper reporter, I found my perceived dual identity to be both useful and funny. I once telephoned a black editor at an African-American newspaper about doing a freelance story for them, and he declared proudly that his publication would be "happy to consider a white writer." Every black mainstream-English speaker has stories of making business arrangements on the phone and then — surprise! — getting a different response in person. Hurt feelings, and sometimes lawsuits, result.

It goes further. Middle-class African Americans who speak mainstream English are sometimes seen as Uncle Toms by other blacks, who may view the very act of such speech as "giving in" to the coercion of white society. Among many poor black youths, the idea of any access to the mainstream has become a bitter joke, and speaking standard English is grounds for immediate ridicule for one's having surrendered to the white man's rules. Meanwhile, in the ears of white suburbia, the very sound of black English, with its lowered pitch and rounded-off consonants and high-flung vowels, becomes a trumpet of illiteracy and criminality — or, to the young, a siren song of danger and rebellion. As with past generations of white youths, black talk — today it's the hip-hop vocabulary — is a verbal badge of being edgy and cool.

Language, like artillery, carries a charge. And we aim it, however unintentionally, at one another's heads. When we make assumptions about one another on subways and in stores and in offices, much more is at stake than mere speech.

If you can remember, think back to the mid-1990s flare-up over Ebonics. The flames first erupted when the Oakland, California, school board voted to recognize Ebonics (a name contrived by combining *ebony* with *phonics*) as the primary language of African-American students. Rocket explosions ensued. Prominent black intellectuals, including Harvard scholar Henry Louis Gates Jr. and poet and author Maya Angelou, lined up to torpedo the idea. Others rushed forward to defend it. Amid the uproar, the Oakland board softened ("clarified" was the official word) its position, and in the end the board's Ebonics gambit looked for all the world much more like an imaginative bid for badly needed funding than a philosophical stand for the black vernacular.

But in its vehemence, the debate laid bare the essential issue for many African Americans in this business of "good" and "bad" speech: the need to defend the beleaguered black psyche against the weapon of language.

It is an old story, but one that has still not registered with most Americans. Just as wars, such as the Norman Conquest in England, have throughout history broken previous linguistic ties by imposing a conqueror's tongue, so did the forced dislocation of West Africans to the New World undermine black identity by attacking the languages that expressed it. Slave owners learned early that controlling their "property" meant outlawing African languages (as well as African music and cultural traditions). Slaves were literally and figuratively battered with the message that African speech was not only backward but criminal, and that the language and culture of white Americans were superior. Slaves rebelled by using secret systems of speech, often as code, that preserved aspects of African languages, and combined them with vernacular, often regional English. It was an act of creativity that continues to this day. So does the unmistakable mainstream message that white speech patterns and cultural behavior are more desirable than black ones.

To a greater extent than white Americans, African Americans understand explicitly that speaking "white" English is a prerequisite to being taken seriously (outside of pop music and the NBA) by mainstream America. Blacks also understand that speaking "black" English is more or less a guarantee of being stereotyped as poor, ignorant, and possibly dangerous. While analogous in some ways, the experiences of other immigrant groups are very different in that they lack the legacies of slavery and racial segregation. Irish Americans, for instance, were maligned and oppressed in their early years here and even occasionally lynched, but never knew the systematic discrimination of Jim Crow, the huge scale of lynchings experienced by blacks, or the indelible brand of inferiority by skin color. Ultimately they were more able to merge with the mainstream, shedding their traditional speech on the way.

None of this, of course, is absolute: people of all backgrounds hold on to pieces of traditional vernacular. But having options makes all the difference. For many black Americans, for whom traditional paths of assimilation have been blocked — first by blanket discrimination and then by a lack of jobs and funding for public education — the resentment for being ridiculed as an isolated subculture runs deep. And I mean deep. To many African Americans, being mocked for speaking black English — a favorite stunt of such Rage Radio personalities as Rush Limbaugh — feels like being called a savage all over again.

The result is what you might expect. In many poor black communities today, children who speak mainstream English, or who embrace scholarship and the idea of upward mobility, are derided by other black kids for "acting white." Within the college-educated African American middle class, so-called mainstream English is embraced (with varying degrees of grammatical correctness) as standard speech. At the same time, most black middle-class Americans, like me, hold on to black English as a way of being "down" among other black folk, using black expressions and inflections to cement the cultural bonds we share. But having become, in effect, bilingual, middle-class blacks sometimes take umbrage when a nonblack stranger assumes that they speak only black English.

The amount of typecasting African Americans encounter is beyond belief. Once, for example, I hired a video production company in another city to do some work for one of my advertising clients. As routinely happens in advertising production, I hired them sight unseen, choosing them on the strength of their previous work and our numerous telephone conversations. Finally, the time came for us to meet in person at their facility. I was in charge of the entire enterprise, and was accompanied on the trip by a white producer, whom I had also hired. The company representative, who was white, greeted us in the lobby by extending his hand enthusiastically to the white producer and calling him by my name. After weeks of phone conversations, he was utterly confident that this was the man who had hired him. And he was utterly embarrassed when he learned otherwise. Like so many others, he had racial preconceptions about authority. And without the cue of "black" speech on the telephone, he was lost.

Small daily assumptions are just as common. White salespeople and gas station attendants and doormen cock their heads to a black man with, "Help you, yo?" after having saluted a white customer, "Have a nice day, sir." White receptionists spell out directions to the eighth floor with exaggerated slowness, as if translating English for the uninitiated. It is a routine ordeal of laughable absurdity. After all, would a white clerk who greets a black man with "Help you, yo?" also greet an Asian customer by mimicking a Chinese accent?

But there are other, deeper questions here. How should we treat black English when we hear it? Should we take the idea of "black English" as a formal tongue seriously? Standard American English is, after all, not much closer to the King's English than Ebonics. I once heard a novelist observe, in talking about the peculiarities of American language, that the French version of his latest book carried the inscription "translated from the American" (as opposed to "the English"). All languages evolve continuously. And linguists agree that there is an unmistakably systematic structure to black English. A commonly cited example (this one is from linguist John R. Rickford) is its five forms of the present tense: "He runnin' " ("He is running"), "He be runnin' " ("He is usually running"), "He be steady runnin' " ("He is usually running in an intensive, sustained manner"), "He bin runnin' " ("He has been running"), and "He BIN runnin' " ("He has been running for a long time and still is"). Given all of this, and the historical reasons why black English has been ghettoized, shouldn't we be willing to recognize it as an official language?

I think it is the wrong question. While linguists continue to debate the nature of black English (most agree it is a dialect), the fact remains that it is a form of nonstandard English, in a nation in which "standard" English is the rule. And by that measure, much of black English — like the English spoken by many uneducated whites — is poor English. There is no racial element in a white person saying to her white boss, "Where you gonna be at?" or "I ain't got none." She speaks that way because she has not learned to speak otherwise. To the extent that she is allowed to remain untutored in standard English, her opportunities in life will suffer, just as they do for millions of African Americans.

We do children no favors by assigning official status to a vernacular when what they really need, beyond their everyday speech, is mastery of the language of the wider society. For us to accept any goal short of competency in standard English — being bilingual, if you like — flies in the face of common sense. The important questions for us to ask are these: Why are inner-city schools being allowed to crumble? Why are employment markets in black communities perpetually at depression levels, sapping students of any hope for jobs and careers? And, as I once heard an African-American scholar ask, why are so many black children closing ranks, in their language and their values, within a cynical subculture that is increasingly isolated from, and hostile toward, the mainstream?

I was raised by college-educated parents, both of whom were reared in the North. Both speak "standard" English with no recognizable "black" accent; not surprisingly, so do I. This is not an affect. I came by it naturally, as did my parents, both of whose families spoke in this manner. Speaking in this way does not make me better or smarter or more sophisticated than a speaker of black English. It has, however, given me choices about how to make myself understood. It has extended my communicative reach. And isn't that why we have language?

Black or white, you can appreciate the history, depth, and beauty of black English while insisting on fluency in standard English. We needn't treat it as a proposition of professor-talk versus felon-talk. If you're white, listen to black English as you would any dialect, and hear the keen colors and meanings it brings to the language, its creativity and precision. Hip-hop, as an art form, has popularized the profound creativity of black English like never before. Why can't standard English rest right alongside black English, just as gracefully, on the same tongue? Here, for example, is celebrated African-American novelist Zora Neale Hurston, from her 1937 masterpiece *Their Eyes Were Watching God*:

> [Pheoby said,] "Most of dese zigaboos is so het up over yo' business till they liable to hurry theyself to Judgment to find out about you if they don't soon know. You better make haste and tell 'em 'bout you and Tea Cake gittin' married, and if he taken all yo' money and went off wid some young gal, and where at he is now and where at is all yo' clothes dat you got to come back here in overhalls."

And here is Hurston again, on the very next page:

> They sat there in the fresh young darkness close together. Pheoby eager to feel and do through Janie, but hating to show her zest for fear it might be thought mere curiosity. Janie full of that oldest human longing — self-revelation. Pheoby held her tongue for a long time, but she couldn't help moving her feet. So Janie spoke.[1]

There was only one Zora Neale Hurston. There are as many more potential colors of speech as there are African

Americans or whites or Hispanics or Asians. Spend time with the verse of African-American poet Yusef Komunyakaa (his *Neon Vernacular* collection won the Pulitzer Prize), and his orchestra of voices will leave your ears ringing. Read the novels of Susan Straight (including *The Gettin' Place* and *Blacker Than a Thousand Midnights*), which vividly portray the interior of black life and language. She's white. Or check out African-American critic and columnist Greg Tate, author of *Flyboy in the Buttermilk* and editor of *Everything but the Burden,* a collection of essays about white appropriation of black culture, who blends black vernacular with other influences in an intellectually fierce style all his own. All of these writers have distinctive messages and singular voices. If you came to their work with any preconception of how a "black voice" is supposed to sound, you would miss the mark by miles. Every time.

The same applies to everyday language. If you are white, understand that use of black English says no more and no less about the speaker's character than your speech says about yours. If you are black, understand that the same applies to standard English. Yes, some blacks are ashamed of their blackness and try to "act white" by denying their heritage in a variety of ways. But merely being fluent in a language — be it standard English or Chinese — is no measure of a person. To make such a judgment, you have to look more deeply into their behavior and beliefs.

In any case, never presume to try to "speak someone's language" based on their appearance. In casual encounters, speak in your normal manner unless you have a compelling reason to do otherwise — say, while traveling in Spain. Avoid making assumptions about ethnicity from phone conversations, unless a specific accent is so unmistakable as to put the matter beyond doubt. Even then you could be wrong. And the conversational hole you will have to dig yourself out of may be deep. As a black American who is often greeted face-to-face with such foolish attempts at "translation," I find the best response is to simply reply in my ordinary way of speaking. This straightens people up quickly.

Whatever your race, you have no right to pipe up and correct the grammar of an adult unless you have reason to believe that your input will be constructive and welcomed. As for correcting a child's speech, it must be done, if at all, by the child's own parent, guardian, or teacher. It is not your place to step in and play grammarian unless you know that the parent would wish you to do so.

My own favorite summary of the black English controversy comes from Henry Louis Gates Jr., who joked about how his own father declared that the entire black English quarrel was "modiculous" and that he was "regusted" with the whole thing. Sadly, however, the fiery debate over black English ultimately misses the point. What black communities really need are the money, support, and resources to teach a generation of increasingly alienated African-American children.

When are we as a nation going to have the mettle to talk that kind of talk?

Survival Suggestions

1. Never try to talk "their" kind of English to a stranger. Ever.

Approaching a black stranger with your attempt at "black" speech, or making the equivalent assumption about anyone based on their ethnicity, is one of the most flagrant insults possible. Don't do it. Period. Show people the common courtesy of assuming that they will understand your normal speech. Then, if they don't, you can take it from there.

2. Never make ethnic assumptions based on telephone conversations.

This is not only offensive, it also puts you at risk of big-time embarrassment. In certain very clear-cut cases — for instance, if you are Russian and you hear an accent of a Russian dialect that you think you recognize — you might ask, but even then only if it is relevant. On the telephone, assume that you will not know a person's ethnicity unless you meet her, or unless the conversation requires that you ask her.

3. If someone insults you by trying to talk "your" talk, correct him.

People need to learn that they ought not treat others in this way. If someone offends you in this manner, one way to set him straight is to look him in the eye and reply in an accentuated form of your normal speech. Another is to flat-out tell him that he shouldn't make assumptions about how you speak. Handle it as you wish. But make certain that he gets the message.

16

Telling Ethnic Jokes: Do You Dare?

A black man walks into a bar with a parrot
on his shoulder. The bartender says, "Hey,
where'd you get that?" The parrot says,
"Africa."

— A joke making the rounds

. . . And that's why darkies were born.

— Groucho Marx, at the end of a frenzied
monologue in the film *Duck Soup*

Black jokes. Jewish jokes. Polish jokes. They are awful. They are demeaning. They are racist and divisive. They are unforgivable. And in just the right context and the right company, some of them are funny. Every black person, every Jew, every Pole — except for those who have boiled away their capacity for irony — knows this. And that's the problem. Because while we may be more than willing to laugh at ourselves in the warmth of safe company, we are not willing to fling wide the doors and invite others to laugh at us. We know that what might be a wicked little joke in our own self-protective hands is, in the hands of someone who does not mean well, a weapon.

You could call this two-sided attitude toward jokes hypocrisy. I call it survival. When popular culture or the media and entertainment industries indulge in racial or ethnic stereotype, the injured parties naturally resist by trying to take charge of their own image. At the same time, they reserve the right to poke at their own innards, or even to diss themselves unmercifully.

Q: How do you stop black kids from jumping up and
   down on the bed?
A: Put Velcro on the ceiling.

When one of my sisters, whose black self-esteem and love of children are unshakable, leaned over conspiratorially years ago and told me that joke, we both laughed and winced. We laughed not because we like to demean black children but because we are incapable of doing so. Because we were once black children ourselves, grimacing as our mother pulled a plastic comb through our oiled hair. Because, to our eyes, nothing can stop a nappy-headed black kid from being beautiful. Least of all the outrageous image of being stuck momentarily to the ceiling.

But when a white man with a fake mustache and an unlit cigar turns to the camera, as Groucho Marx does in *Duck Soup,* to deliver a throwaway line about "darkies," I do not laugh. Nor have I ever, in all of the times I have seen that classic film, heard anyone else laugh at that line. A quick put-down from a smart-assed white man, who knows or cares little about actual black people, is not funny. It's just plain old racism.

To be fair to Groucho, he came straight out of vaudeville, which also produced Al Jolson, and he worked in an era in which stereotype was king. In the late 1930s and '40s, when black actress Hattie McDaniel was considered a glittering success for having played the faithful rag-headed maid, Mammy, in the movie *Gone with the Wind,* making "darkie" jokes and staging chorus scenes of dancing black cotton pickers (as in the Marx Brothers film *A Day at the Races*) was considered solid entertainment for white audiences. I doubt, however, that blacks laughed at those scenes then. And I hear no whites laughing now.

When it comes to ethnic jokes, thoughtful people should entertain a kind of unofficial etiquette. They may not always follow it, but they should embrace it. Call it the Masturbation Rule: When it comes to indulging in ethnic humor, the privilege of self-abuse belongs, ultimately, to the affected group alone. All others, while they may dare to chortle over the foibles of the Polish or Jewish or black guy who walks into a bar, do so at their own bloody peril. It is a good rule.

A predominantly Jewish or heavily black audience

howls at a Jewish or black stand-up comic's ethnic "inside" joke because it understands. Mixed with the humor, however cruel, is knowledgeable empathy and unthreatened self-esteem. If as an outsider you lack this understanding, your laughter becomes literally oppressive. Show me a white person telling a "black" joke with no black person in sight, and I'll show you a person who likely has few or no black friends, who has almost no personal knowledge of black people, who is probably not comfortable being around black people, and who, worse, believes that her own racial ignorance and discomfort are perfectly acceptable.

That's what is wrong with some of the so-called black television characters and sitcoms that amuse so many of us. The sassing, gassing, sashaying, mutually dissing "black" characters of many prime-time black comedy shows, from *Amos 'n' Andy* to *Booty Call* and beyond, have been, in effect, a "black" joke told by white-dominated media, with the help of career-savvy black stars and writers and producers willing to cash in. Viewers, game for familiar formulas and easy laughs, have gotten the same mouth-flapping black brothers and sarcastic black sisters in show after show, all justified by marketing surveys indicating that of the (few) options available, black viewers pick these. Things have, thankfully, improved in recent years; there is a broader range of black life, both funny and dramatic, on TV, and comedians Chris Rock and Dave Chappelle, in particular, have brought outrageously clever and irreverent ethnic humor to television. But there is still far too much minstrelsy in the choices we have.

It's not that we should replace the formulaic shows with antiseptic politically approved skits. And it's not that

the jokes on these cookie-cutter shows are never funny. It's
that there is not a black voice — the voice of a broader variety of black experience — doing the telling. And, for me,
it is hard to laugh at "nigger" jokes told by white television executives — even with black actors or screenwriters
as mouthpieces.

But wait. I hear a white person objecting: "Why all of
the carrying on about black humor? You've admitted that
everyone is a fair target for ethnic jokes: Jews, Italians,
Poles, Scandinavians. This is America. We're all cartoon
characters. What's the big deal?"

Well, see, the thing is, we are not all cartoon characters. I challenge you to tell me one "white" joke. I don't
mean a joke about a specific ethnic or cultural or subgen-
der group of whites — WASPs, Poles, Germans, hillbillies,
blonds. I mean a joke that makes fun of the broad, generally understood American idea of being white. In the same
way that a "black" joke makes fun of the very idea of
being black. Have you heard many such "white" jokes recently? I'll bet you haven't. Because, as we have all had
drummed into us, most frequently by television, "whiteness" is not, in and of itself, remarkable or funky or quaint.
Whiteness is therefore not funny. It is featureless. It is invisible. It is the norm.

Tell a Polish joke, any Polish joke, even the most vul-
gar one imaginable. When you have finished, and the
laughter has faded, the Polish farmer in the punch line
strolls out of the joke and back onto the street, where he
melds into the blanket identity of whiteness. In the sidewalk crowd, he is no longer seen as the butt of a Polish
joke. He is a white guy. But what about the guy in the
black joke? What about the black guy with the parrot on

his shoulder? When he escapes the punch line and strolls onto the street, he is still seen as the character in the joke: a guy dumb enough to be led around by a bird. He cannot merge with the throng of "normalcy." He remains separate, noticed, "a black guy." And everybody knows what *that* means.

This is the setting within which you or I or anyone tells a "black joke." No wonder, then, that to some African Americans any humor at their expense is unacceptable, and any such humor expressed by a black person is treason. And no wonder that many of us have strict rules of engagement for such jokes, even when they happen to make us laugh. We know the damage that they can do in unfriendly hands. And that's not funny.

Hence the Masturbation Rule: Abuse yourself up to the limits of what you are able to tolerate and defend. Abuse others at your own profound risk. Which means, if you're black, you can tell a "black" joke and, at the very worst, expect to fight or talk your way out of it. And if you're white, you cannot.

It is a good rule because it rests on ownership. The state of being black belongs to black people, and if you are an African American your particular state of being black belongs to you. No one, black or white, can define the terms of your racial self-respect. No one can decree that you can't laugh at such-and-such and still like yourself, or that you can't say so-and-so and still love being black. It's your call to make. If you decide that your identity can handle the tension of chuckling at a sinfully awful black joke, laugh. And be prepared for accusations of blasphemy.

If you are white, blackness is not yours to abuse in

the first place. Unless you are so comfortable with African-American friends that you know you can take such liberties among them, keep your hands off of black jokes. Maybe you simply cannot resist the naughty little pleasure; if so, the mere transgression doesn't make you a racist. But do you have any black friends? Do you hang around with African Americans enough to know anything firsthand about black life? Or is your image of black people a collection of sitcom fragments, NBA games, and observations from across subway platforms? If you snicker at a punch line while remaining ignorant about African Americans, you have made a joke of racial understanding itself. And that is a worse crime than all the black jokes in the world.

Survival Suggestions

1. Observe the Masturbation Rule.

It's easy to remember: The privilege of self-abuse belongs to the affected group alone. If you don't belong to that group, you don't get to tell the joke. And even if you do belong, you tell the joke at your own peril. And take your licks. Break the rule, and you had better be prepared for whatever reaction you get.

2. Don't be afraid to object to a mean joke.

Particularly if you're white, peer pressure and Rage Talk contempt for cultural respect may make it seem intimidating to raise your objection to a joke you don't like, especially among friends or coworkers. But that is exactly when it needs to happen. What better lesson to a mean-spirited joke teller than to hear disapproval from someone she considers a peer? Speak up. Use your influence where it counts. At the very least, the teller will more carefully consider her audience next time, and perhaps reflect on that type of humor as well.

Just Between Us

17

What's Wrong with "Tolerance"?

T olerance.

It is a word that has helped to persuade millions of human beings to treat one another in a more civilized manner.

It is part of the name of a curriculum, now offered to schools nationwide, that teaches children to have greater awareness of and consideration toward one another's cultures and characteristics.

It has improved a national vocabulary that previously offered only such terms as integration *and* assimilation *and* diversity *as attempts to express the more profound idea of appreciating our differences.*

It has moved the ball forward in how we as Americans relate to one another.
So what's not to like about it?

What's not to like about *tolerance* is that, as a choice of terms for interaction, it is anchored too much in the old idea of mutual indulgence and not enough in the more constructive idea of active embrace.

Tolerance falls short of what we humans need to be doing in sharing a nation or sharing a planet. I don't like *tolerance* as a beacon to follow, and I never have. I'll tell you why.

Tolerance is a physical capacity one acquires for an addictive drug. *Tolerance* is a response cultivated toward an acquaintance who has chronic body odor. *Tolerance* is what you show toward a neighbor's child who daily makes excruciating sounds trying to learn to play the violin.

Tolerance subtly reinforces the idea that it is sufficient for us merely to put up with one another. *Tolerance* requires that we behave with dignity and consideration toward one another, but it leaves room for us to internally retain our biases and our inclinations to make culturally centric judgments. *Tolerance* demands that we do a certain amount of important and positive external work, but it does not necessarily insist that we do our internal work.

To be sure, the best approaches to tolerance can, in fact, encourage both our external and internal work. The word itself does not forbid our going beyond good behavior to address the deeper issues of understanding why our quality of experience is no better than anyone else's. But it does not *require* it, either. *Tolerance*, left to its own devices, leaves too much potentially biased wiggle room. It leaves room for us to smile politely at our differences while still walking away feeling internally superior. It allows a straight person to act congenially and professionally toward a gay coworker while holding on to an internal bias against homosexuality. It allows a black person to smile his way through a meal prepared by a Korean friend and then walk away marveling to himself at how "those people don't know how to cook."

The point isn't that you have to *like* a meal from an unfamiliar cuisine, or that you need to try to become gay (as if that were possible) in order to appreciate your coworker. The point, instead, is that there is nothing inherently more likeable or more normal about one or the other. There are infinite varieties of goodness and normalcy, and yours is just one. Mere *tolerance* can skip this essential realization.

So we need more than *tolerance*.

And that is why I suggest another word: *respect*.

Respect is the dynamic, deliberate embrace of the validity of other people's experiences and cultures and orientations. It goes a step beyond the perceived kindness of *tolerance* and fulfills the deeper moral obligation to understand that our lives as humans are qualitatively equal: not the same (how could they be?), but *of equal quality*. Respect is the act of living this understanding, both through one's behavior and through one's evolving beliefs.

So I suggest that you and I move beyond tolerance and into active respect. Respect is what will enable us to acknowledge our differences, and even to laugh at them, while enjoying our underlying bond of appreciation for the validity of one another's personhood. Respect is what will enable you to eat food that seems strange to you, and perhaps even register your queasiness if you have a comfortable enough relationship with your host, while sharing a mutual confidence that the two of you have true regard for each other's customs and tastes. Respect is what will allow you to experience moral or political disagreements without feeling that you either have to agree or keep quiet.

It needs to be said, of course, that neither *tolerance* nor *respect* ought to be used as rationalizations for condoning cruel, criminal, or harmful conduct. A person who abuses a spouse or molests a child or mistreats an animal cannot hide beneath the shield of cultural relativism. And there will be conflicts in which it is necessary for one culture to clash with accepted tenets of another out of a commitment to human justice. The global fight to end the genital mutilation of women in certain cultures is one such case. Respect for differing points of view does not exempt us from acting on our consciences, and most of us, if we have truly embraced the idea of respect, can recognize the extremes at which we need to draw our lines in the sand.

In the meantime, let's thank tolerance for its years of valuable service, and move on to the more rewarding realm of respect.

Survival Suggestions

1. Know the difference between tolerance and respect.

Think about what it means to tolerate differences between you and another person. Then contrast that with what it means to respect those differences. When you hear people warmly advocate tolerance, watch and listen closely. What do they actually mean? Do they express their appreciation of difference through mere friendly coexistence, or do they dig more deeply for mutual respect? Let the latter be your standard for dealing with difference.

2. Expect respect. Of yourself, and of others.

If you are not granting true respect toward people whose cultures, genders, religions, sexual orientations, or experiences differ from yours, begin to do so. This deserves some thought and struggle on your part. Don't let yourself get away with simple tolerance. You wouldn't want to feel merely tolerated, and neither do others. In that vein, if someone else does not treat you with true respect on these issues of difference, expect (and demand if you need to) that he do so. Fair is fair.

18

Picking Your Spots: When Is It Worth It to Speak Up?

our true stories:
One evening at a very nice hotel where I was staying, I went downstairs to have dinner in the restaurant. As it happened, there was a convention at the hotel, and the restaurant lobby was packed with people waiting to be seated. I asked the hostess how long the wait would be, had her add my name to the list, and then stood around waiting with everyone else. I was nondescriptly dressed, like most other guests. But within a few minutes, a white man approached me with his group of friends. "How long will the wait be for a table?" he asked me cordially. I looked at him evenly. "I don't know," I replied.

"You'll need to ask somebody on the restaurant staff. I'm a guest, like you." He gave a start. "Oh!" he said sheepishly. "I'm sorry. I thought you worked here." I cocked my head, looked at him quizzically, and asked, "Why did you think that?" He stared at me, mouth open, trying to move his lips to answer. There was nothing he could say. But the answer to my question was clear to him. And to me.

After midnight one morning, my girlfriend and I were sitting in the waiting room of an all-night emergency veterinarian's office, awaiting attention for my sick cat. Also in the room were a female couple with their frisky black Lab, and a woman with a dachshund. When the dachshund woman's turn came to see the vet, she stood, walked to the apparently gay couple, and said, "Jesus hates the sin but loves the sinner. I ask God to forgive you." She then turned and headed for the examination room. The gay couple, shocked and speechless, stared at her as she walked away. I, trying lamely to think fast, called out at the woman, "You didn't need to say that!" My girlfriend, who had been reading, asked me, "What did she say?" "She said something very stupid," I replied, loudly enough that I hoped the dachshund woman overheard me. The gay couple, unruffled, assured me that they were okay. I sat back and calmed down, feeling that I did not have the right to draw this couple unwillingly into a public scene. But I sure wished that the dachshund woman had been left with something to chew on. Later, at home, my girlfriend came up with a zinger: I could have told the offending Bible-thumper, "I hope God forgives YOU." I wish I had said it when I had the chance. Next opportunity I have, I will.

During my childhood in the 1960s, our household pro-
vided, to many in the surrounding community of middle-
class whites, hard actual evidence that black folk did not
reside in trees. Once, my mother and a white neighbor
were in the middle of a mildly political conversation when
the white woman suddenly put down her coffee cup,
peered earnestly at my mother, and asked, "Why am I
afraid of black people?" My mother looked serenely back
at her. "Because you're a racist," she answered.

A friend of mine, who is white, has a sister-in-law who is
black. One day, my friend, who as it happens has a long
history of sending cute animal greeting cards to her brother,
picked out a typically precious card featuring a photo-
graph of an orangutan. Since she knew the couple was ex-
pecting a child, she inscribed the card with a whimsical
message to her brother about his impending fatherhood.
She mailed the card. Days later, her black sister-in-law
telephoned, furious: "How dare you send a card with a
monkey on it!"

Memories of high-school science notwithstanding (orang-
utans are apes, not monkeys), I was of no help to my friend
after she finished telling me her story. She was pained; I was
laughing. Her questions for me were: (1) Had she been in-
sensitive? and (2) How in the world was she ever going to
pick out another card for this woman? My only question,
which I tried to put tactfully, was whether the sister-in-law
was in therapy, and if not, why not.

Four very different stories, involving different situations and feelings. In the first, a white person makes a casually offensive assumption about a black stranger and is

embarrassed when he is rightly forced to examine it. In the second, a person brazenly makes a bigoted personal judgment of two gay women, and a bystander grapples with how to come to the gay women's defense without compromising their right to control the incident. In the third, a white person dares to bare feelings she is ashamed of, and a black person dares to reply truthfully at the risk of poisoning a friendly relationship. In the fourth, a black person lashes out, offended, and the shocked white person struggles to react, torn between self-doubt and common sense. At least three of the four are fairly dramatic incidents, but equivalents of all four situations happen all the time.

All four raise the same questions: In an era as fear-laden as ours today, how do we confront bigotry in others and in ourselves? And in situations involving people we know, how do we lay it on the line to one another, as people who differ in a million potential ways, without exposing ourselves to merciless shame or, worse, walking into personal warfare?

Correcting a stranger's bigoted presumption is relatively easy, more a matter of tactics and the luck of quick thinking than anything else. I was happy to have come up with the line I used with the white stranger in the restaurant. I was frustrated by my inability to think of something more effective to say to the bigoted woman in the vet's office, although the reply my girlfriend came up with later is one that I've stored away for future use and that I recommend to you as well. Another thing I learned from the vet-office encounter, pointed out to me by one of my sisters, is that I, as a person who has gay relatives and close friends, could have taken the initiative to directly confront the woman's bigoted attitude as a personal affront to my own values and loved ones. This was a judgment call, since the two gay women appeared to not want to be part of a huge scene. In such situations, we often need to make quick decisions about boldness and discretion.

But how do you know when to tell your well-meaning white neighbor that she is a racist, or when to tell your black sister-in-law that she is paranoid?

The answer is that if we all waited until we knew we were right before opening our mouths, allowing ourselves zero risk of misunderstanding or overstatement, then necessary conversations would never happen. We have to face it: change requires risk. There are leaps to be made, conversational licks to be taken. What has so many well-intentioned white and black people either stammering or seething is the half-witted notion that we cannot afford to be racially in error, cannot afford to be corrected, cannot abide conflict or argument and still sustain a healthy coexistive relationship.

So once conversation has been sufficiently stifled — as it has today by public Rage Talk and private eye-rolling — there is really only one way through: what I call "engagement." You have to risk being taken for a judgmental white racist or an apologist for black dysfunction. Maybe that's what you actually are. Maybe you deserve to have it flung back in your face. Perhaps you need a good rocking and rolling, a healthy little bang of criticism. Or maybe, the other party should not be spared what you hold clenched in your fist. Perhaps somebody needs to be called out. And perhaps, when all is said and done, everyone survives.

My mother's white friend could have taken the easy way out. She did not have to admit to a black person that she was afraid of black people. And she certainly did not have to be willing to explore the reason why. She could have done what a million white people would have done: smiled, finished her coffee without comment, and counted the money in her purse the minute my mother left. Instead, she took a personal risk and spoke up. So did my mother, who, rather than smoothing over a horribly awkward moment with a conciliatory reply, plunged straight into the ugly heart of the matter. The resulting conversation taught them both something about unexpected potential. Over the ensuing years, they never became close friends. But they probably never would have anyway. The point is that their brutal honesty on that day did not end their relationship. It may have even helped to sustain it.

Not that happy endings are assured. As I said, this is all about risk. I cannot imagine the orangutan affair ending with anything like harmony, let alone hugs. And yet, it had to happen the way it did. The white woman, having a perfectly happy history of sending animal cards to her brother, never even thought about race. The black sister-in-law's incensed reply caught the white woman at her most vulnerable point: her awareness that she does not know what it feels like to be black. She was trapped. Her instincts told her that her sister-in-law was being ridiculous. But her fear of being shamed as a racist prevented her from trusting herself: "What if I'm wrong? What if she had a right to be offended? How can I know for certain?"

In fact, she could not know for sure. When she got the angry phone call, she had to make a decision based on uncertainty. She could trust herself and take the heat: "Orangutan? Nigger joke? Excuse me? Woman, what *are* you talking about?" Or she could disobey her instincts and fold: "I didn't mean it that way. I apologize." Either way, she risked making a mistake. There was no protection, no guarantee.

But that is precisely the reason to engage. The reality is inescapable: most of the time, you simply cannot know in advance whether you will end up being right or wrong. You cannot know whether you will improve the prospects for friendship or make an enemy. There are too many surprises hidden within racial dialogue. And so the only thing to do is to try, and to accept the risks — of hard feelings, of racial blunders — as being the cost of a process that, in the long run, draws us closer together.

One night years ago at a Thai restaurant in Amsterdam, a waiter was about to seat me when the maître d' hastily interfered. He pointed ruefully to his watch: it was ten o'clock, he said. Closing time. He was sorry, but very firm. He could seat no more customers. I was hungry. I was alone. I looked around at the room packed with European faces, and I snapped back bitterly, automatically, "Would it be closed if I were *white*?" The maître d' stared dumbly at me for a moment, and then he suddenly saw how the pieces fit and he smiled, saying gently, "No, oh no, I am not like that. It's not what you think." His sincerity was unassailable. He asked me if I would please come back tomorrow; he promised I would not be disappointed. I felt a sickening sense of embarrassment at myself. I apologized for my hastiness, and I returned the next night — before ten o'clock — and was rewarded with a fine meal and warm treatment. It's not that there is no racism in Amsterdam. There was plenty of it even then, and today in the post-9/11 era of stereotyping and angry retaliation there is more racism than ever. But I had simply picked the wrong situation in which to

take offense. Had I not made my ill-fated show of indignation, I would never have learned that I was wrong about
that restaurant and, no doubt, wrong about a good deal
more. I carried the lesson back home.

On another occasion, while working as a copywriter
at an advertising agency, I noticed that a particular white
art director with whom I was paired never seemed to include people of color in his ads. The two of us would come
up with an idea for a campaign — with no mention of
race — and when he came back with layouts and TV story-
boards, all of the characters would be white. All of the
time. Finally, I said something about it. He listened. He politely bristled. He said race wasn't the kind of thing he
thought about. He said he didn't see it as an issue. I replied
that it *was* an issue; not everyone in our target audience
was white. He didn't say much in response. Our conversation pretty much ended there. But soon thereafter, people of
color began to appear in his layouts.

I travel and speak a good deal to audiences who are
sometimes hesitant — or cynical — about getting into
racial or ethnic conversations. One of the things that I suggest to people is that we have to demand more from our relationships with one another. Rage Talk culture and the
growing frustration among many about the prospects for
feeling understood (angry whites who feel attacked by
black or Arab complaints, angry blacks who feel their
grievances ignored, angry people of Arab descent who feel
their mistreatment and stigmatization condoned) can bring
people to the point of abandoning any effort to try to be
heard. The implicit feeling is, Why bother? *"They" won't
get it anyway.* I say, however, it is time to straighten our
backs and not be so easily scared off by one another. I think

we need to start being *insistent* about what we need for one another to hear and understand. And we need to be more insistent, as well, about the amount of potential discord and struggle our relationships as fellow citizens can tolerate. I think the glue of survivable coexistence is stronger than we think. If we are going to share a nation and a planet, it had better be.

Get in the game already. Realize that your only hope for any kind of peace with this business of racism is to understand that confrontation need not lead to annihilation. You can survive offending a sister-in-law or a coworker — at least when both conversants lack deadly weapons, which is nearly all of the time, despite the paranoia of our era. You can also survive being wrong, and even learn from it. People will let you know soon enough what they think of what you think. But how do you expect to find out with your mouth closed? Not that you should feel entitled to fling around "Re-Legalize Slavery" or "Castrate White Men" proclamations with the expectation of promoting reasoned dialogue. But at a certain point, like it or not, you will have to trust your own idea of what is reasonable, and go with it.

You are entitled, of course, to pick your spots. You have the right to a life that is not dominated by difficult encounters, arguments, and chancy attempts at understanding. It's your prerogative to choose when it is worth it to you to engage and when it is not. People of color, in particular, tend to be unfairly assigned the societal job of "raising" the hard ethnic issues with whites, and we get sick of it. As the black dean of a college once told me about African-American students at her school who avoid formal group discussions about race, "They get tired of having to be black all the time." Whoever you are, decide when you think dealing with an issue is necessary and worthy of your energy. And then do it.

Do you think that a particular black-made film was shallow and mean-spirited? Say so. Does it seem to you that a certain white shimmy-singer has ascended to the stature of pop deity basically by lip-synching the heartbreak-thin keening of Motown divas past? Out with it. Has a prominent African-American activist made statements that seem absurd to you? Let's hear it. Is television's latest sassy-darkie or sensitive-detective minstrel sitcom more than you can bear? Don't hold back. From what I have seen of racial card-folding among folks who ought to be arguing, the most dangerously racist assumption is that an acquaintance of another ethnicity "won't be able to handle" disagreement or challenge. Please. While zealots are out starting wars, killing civilians, and burning places of worship, the rest of us are afraid to talk because we might *upset* one another?

I say, Let's talk while we still can.

Survival Suggestions

1. Expect more of relationships.

At a certain point, we have to reclaim our relationships, as Americans of all colors, from the low expectations of today's Rage Talk environment. Realize that disagreement and struggle are survivable in relationships with friends, neighbors, and coworkers as long as it is handled within the bounds of reason and mutual respect. You do not have the right to say to your neighbor, "People like you make me sick." (At least, if you plan on sustaining a relationship.) You do have the right to say, "I think you have some ideas about my ethnicity that are wrong, and it really upsets me, and we need to talk about it."

2. Reserve your right to pick your spots.

You have no obligation to spend your entire life correcting bad ideas and addressing misunderstandings. Pick the situations that you need to deal with. Face them. And let the rest go.

3. Don't tolerate casual racial slights.

Ignoring casual racism (for instance, a remark such as "you know how *they* are.") only allows people to repeat it. Say something. If you are lucky enough to come up with a quick comeback, so much the better. In any case, let the person know that their behavior or remark was not okay. People with such ideas need to learn that they won't be tolerated.

19

A State of Being Sorry: The "Nice Black Man" Syndrome

D o you know me?
I am a certain black male who always some-how seems to be apologetic. You may have noticed.
For much of my life, in fact, I have apologized too much. Much too much. This has been pointed out to me by friends and by those not so friendly, both gently and stridently. After denying it for as long as was comfortably possible, I decided to investigate both my own behavior and that of my cultural brothers. In the hallways and on the street, in elevators and in arenas, I began to pay attention. And damned if my critics didn't turn out to be right.

Whether you have noticed or not, there is a certain approval-hungry quality to being black, male, and

repentant — most keenly evident among the genial, edu-
cated black males whom the rest of the world regards as
astonishingly nice guys. It is a manner that has nothing at
all to do with good manners.
Let me tell you what I mean.

I watch us, you see — sometimes dressed in jeans, but usually in suits and ties — I see us, in this long, white entry
corridor, apologizing our way through life, "bobbing and
weaving our way down the street," as I once heard a black
psychologist say: accidentally bumping into someone, especially a white someone, and blurting out the most hur-
ried, heartfelt, and excessive stream of apologies for barely
having brushed an arm or a purse; crossing paths with an
oncoming someone, especially a white someone, and immediately and unconsciously yielding while uttering repentant regrets; expertly maneuvering, staying clear, dancing
through, avoiding and denying the glances of fear and resentment that slashingly remind one of the depth to which
we are mistrusted.

This is no accident, this apoplexy of apologizing, no
product of good home training. Like most of our dearly
held ideas of how to behave, it has to do with our very
stance as black men in this particular place at this particular time.

I watch us graciously and conspicuously thanking an
oblivious waiter for the silverware, then the napkin, then
the water, the bread, the iced tea, the entree, the dessert,
and finally even the check; hurrying to excuse ourselves
when we politely cough or sneeze or clear our throat or
even inaudibly sniff. Apologizing, apologizing: for having
been in the way of someone who was also in our way, for

unintentionally unsettling or startling someone, for having misunderstood a trivial thing that could have been better explained, for having asked the store clerk for the wrong brand of soap when the sign was misleading, for any of a thousand flyspeck foibles.

I watch us, day after day, apologizing all up and down our college-educated behinds as we dolefully make our way through the obstacle courses of our lives. I see us apologizing, when all is said and done, for simply being black and male. I see us apologizing for who we are wrongly perceived to be, and struggling through our unintentionally exaggerated public displays of politeness, to let these misguided white people know, once and for all, that we are nice guys, that we are *all right,* even by the rigorously bland standards of American culture.

After all, we educated black men have good table manners and sound personal principles and Lysol in the bathroom and clean underwear beneath our slacks. We are not, despite the clutching of purses and keys and hip pockets that ripples through a crowd as we pass, going to rob or beat or rape Caucasian descendants of slave owners and indentured servants and immigrants. Whether they believe it or not, we are following paths of our own, paths that will allow them to retain possession of their lives and their property and even their privacy. And the more the clutching at purses and stereotypes persists, the more loudly we acceptance-starved respectable black males often feel the need to apologize for our state of mistaken identity:

Please, look at me. Listen to me. Watch me hold the door for you. Pay attention as I generously tip the waiter. Notice as I come within inches of your purse without showing any inclination whatsoever to rob or accost you.

Hear me speak proper English — educated English, English that speaks of intellectual achievement and seriousness of purpose — as I address you. See me walk past you in a fine suit and climb into a car that only a professional could afford. You still do not see? You do not understand? You cannot make out who I am? Oh, excuse me. I am sorry. I beg your pardon. I'll try again.

What an inner monologue to live with. It takes the childhood lessons of my upbringing and amplifies them to soul-splitting volume: there is no virtue greater than being "nice," no sin more venal than being "not nice." To entertain a nasty or cruel notion about someone, or to take a pig-headed position on a subject, becomes not merely wrong or unfair but, worse, not nice. Niceness is the way in, niceness is the admission card to the mainstream, the antidote to one's own toxicity as a black male in a society that presumes all black males to be poisonous. *Yes, you should be intelligent, you should be ambitious, you should be honorable. But you absolutely* must *be nice.*

And so we spread out across the countryside, we hordes of smart and successful black American men, working so very hard at being nice. By the time we reach adulthood we are nice by instinct, nice by reflex, nice without even meaning to be nice. We are so nice that we forget how to fight, so nice that we forget that the territory within our skins belongs to us, so nice that even a whiff of disapproval from the wider world can send us backpedaling in a catechismic flurry of apology. It is almost as if, with our singular black selves, we take on all of the world's sorriness for racism, sorriness for rage, sorriness for misunderstanding. If we are sorry enough — we seem to say — maybe it will all go away.

We can take a lesson — a thoughtful lesson, one that does not treat suicide and survival as fashion statements, as do some of my middle-class black friends with their BMWs and faux-yo attitudes and backward baseball caps — from the yo boys, the street-corner jail baiters, whose single most liberating reality, amid a life of fostered self-endangerment, is the ability to simply say "Fuck you" to the very culture that so strangles the black middle class. We can take a lesson from our tortured but honest little brothers, who meet the clutching of purses and pockets with smoldering stares that say, *I can use your fear against you.* We can apologize less, save our thanks for deserving waiters, stand our ground more. We can begin to live less for others' understanding of us, and more for our own.

We might find that it feels nice.

So much of this apologizing by black gentlemen, after all, does have to do with lost rage: *No, I am not going to brutalize you, although maybe I should.* It is not that men such as we are strangers to anger. It is that we know anger all too well, and we are not willing to let it dominate our public persona. The more bestial the received stereotype of black men, the stiffer our resolve to override it through mild-mannered respectability. It is, however, a hopelessly lost cause for both black and white, because the rage belongs to us all, and it is not going to go away.

The rage is like a heavy metal, mercury or uranium, that long ago leached into the viscera of black and white Americans on Virginia slave docks and has been part of us ever since, sickening, elusive. I watch us constantly hand it off to one another, like handfuls of roiling poison. A white man buys black slaves and lies to himself about their humanity. Three hundred years later, a black teenager glares at a white driver in traffic. Across town, one white woman tells another that black men are scary. In an office tower a few miles away, a black executive carries himself with exaggerated gentility and propriety.

And what if the very fear displayed by whites of blacks reveals whites' unwitting acceptance of the basis for black rage? Sometimes, when I observe whites grabbing their personal belongings in the presence of African Americans, the entire scene seems a metaphor for a guilty white conscience: the former slaveholder, who once trafficked in stolen human property, now anxiously guarding his possessions from the scrutiny of the freed slave. I wonder if such small acts of defensiveness sometimes betray a subconscious white voice: *If I were black and living in the aftermath of having been enslaved, I'd be mad. I might want to take something back as revenge. Hey, where* is *my wallet, anyway?*

Apologies, apologies: the curse of culpability bouncing around like a contaminated tennis ball. President Bill Clinton being sorry for slavery. President George W. Bush being sorry for nothing. A black man on an elevator being sorry for having been mistaken for a caged predator. Have the centuries-long handoffs done us any good? Are any of us, as a result, any less angry? Any less threatened? Any better paid? Any better understood? Just as our response to the national crisis of race must be national political action, not a show of collective sorrow or innocence, our solution to our daily mini-crises of race must be personal action as well.

Understand me: I am not positing individual action as a convenient personal substitute for politics. I am positing it as being part of politics. The politics of racial conflict do not stop at your doorway. They begin there. We must be pissed off and curious and fearless not from a distance but where it counts: up close, in elevators, in long lines at supermarkets, in the kitchens of in-laws, in conversation and argument, in car repair shops, in subway cars. It is in precisely these countless throwaway encounters — the ones in which we presume real racial contact to be unthinkable — that such contact becomes, in fact, vital.

Imagine: in an elevator, the formerly apologetic black man peers at a nervous white stranger and asks, in a deep and even tone of voice, "What are *you* so afraid of?" Or, as did a black male friend of mine in the face of a purse-clutching white woman, he turns the tables by clasping his own briefcase to his chest in parody of her fear. A white man catches a flash of seemingly racial ire from a black coworker, and rather than backpedaling away from yet another "black thing," he asks him what his problem is. A black woman does the same thing with a white acquaintance. A white woman, caught in the heat of a black youth's defiant glance on the subway, pauses to think beyond her own grip on her bag to imagine what sort of security this bristling child has lost — or never known.

It is not rage that we should be worrying about. A mere century and a half after slavery, with the race issue serving as a national punching bag, we assuredly ought to feel hounded by rage. Among blacks, only the walking dead could be free of anger over race, and among scared whites who see no reason to empathize, resentment is inescapable. How could it be otherwise? Did we really think that blacks and whites could brush one another's skins and feel one another's breath in elevators and on sidewalks, free of pain, while hemorrhaging? If you are a black person, forced in a thousand daily ways to fend off — or succumb to — the continually flying shrapnel of slavery's aftermath, of course you are angry. If you are a white person, sucked into a conflict that began with a crime you personally had nothing to do with, of course you are angry.

The danger is not in our having rage, but in our failing to confront one another in close personal quarters, with weapons safely out of reach. The danger is in our feeling, instead, obligated to be secretive, or to be sorry, or to feign innocence, or to be "nice." As if our racial relationships can bear nothing more. But maybe the truth is that our racial relationships cannot bear so little. And maybe we had better ask more of ourselves in our daily crossing of paths.

If we do not, we might be sorry.

Survival Suggestions

1. If you're black, quit this niceness-as-antidote-to-black-toxicity routine.

Just quit it. If you are a black man who, like many, feels hounded by others' fears and underestimations of you, I suggest you do two things. First, cut their hounds loose and lose them. Second, get a hold of some hounds of your own to defend your ability to be who you are: a man with a right to both feel rage and demand respect. The preemptive exaggerated niceness routine will never cure what ails some whites in their view of black men, because their attitude is not about *you* personally and cannot be eradicated by your personal behavior. Plus, this soft-black-man act will kill you before you're sixty. Ditch it.

2. If you're white, quit expecting antiseptic sterility in professional black men.

Just quit it. If you don't demand such softness in white or other nonblack men as assurance of their professionalism and respectability, why should you subconsciously expect it of a black man? Your underlying stereotype of black men as being vaguely threatening is both uncalled-for and unfair to your black professional peers and superiors. Lose it.

20

"Learn Three Facts and Start Yelling": The Updated Ten Most Bigoted Ideas Held by Black and White Americans

M uch has happened since I wrote the original "Ten Worst Racial Ideas" lists in the first edition of Race Manners. We have seen 9/11, the vote-counting controversies in the 2000 and 2004 presidential elections, the determination of a presidency by the U.S. Supreme Court, the rise of both the gay marriage movement and the movement to ban it, the Iraq War, Hurricane Katrina, the second consecutive appointment of a black secretary of state, and much more. This time around, in the wake of these events and others, I have broadened the lists to include simply the "Ten Most Bigoted" ideas of whites and blacks; when you peruse the lists, I think you'll see why I did this.

The phrase "Learn Three Facts and Start Yelling"

comes from the political cartoonist Tom Tomorrow, who has used it as an apt illustration of the dumbness of some current American articles of faith. Some items, being particularly enduring bad ideas, I have carried over from the previous Ten Worst lists. I offer the same caveat as before: These lists are compiled purely on the authority of personal observation, with absolutely no application whatsoever of the scientific method. Objectivity is not guaranteed.

The Ten Most Bigoted Ideas
Held by White Americans

1. Gay marriage will weaken and undermine the institution of holy matrimony.

For sheer absurdity and hatefulness, this popular nugget of bigotry trumps even the worst of whites' wackiest racial and ethnic ideas. Think about it: A straight married couple in Cleveland or Phoenix or Philadelphia fears that the marital union of two gay people anywhere on the continent will somehow dynamite the love, divinity, and meaning inherent in their own existing marriage. Either a lot of heterosexuals are huddling in very shaky marriages, or their unwillingness to share divine grace with other sexual unions betrays a selfishness so hideous that it makes one wonder if God might now withhold the holy blessing of *straight* marriages on the grounds that heterosexuals are too mean to deserve it.

2. Islamic terrorists "hate America because they hate freedom."

This line continues to get great media play, but I've always wondered how many white Americans actually buy it. It's a patently idiotic notion that collapses into dust when one turns off the Fox News Network. Sorry, but what those groups who hate America in the Middle East and Asia want *is* freedom: freedom from American hegemony over their economies and American veto power over their political systems, freedom from American cultural dominance, freedom from American support of the injustices of the Israeli occupation of Palestine, and, most recently, freedom from American invasion and occupation.

3. Black Americans want to feel victimized.

This venerable misconception continues to elude and deny the facts of black life. What a great way for a white person to avoid the real issues of racism: discrimination, double standards in criminal prosecution, poverty, health care, education, police brutality, hate and violence, high blood pressure. As if black people *want* to walk the earth with significantly higher rates of inadequate education, imprisonment, homelessness, heart attack, stroke, diabetes, and general stress and unhappiness. Even to the extent that some blacks do plunge into obsessive race hate, they — like white supremacists — constitute a minority whose psychological desperation does not truly qualify as a "choice" anyway.

4. When it comes to black people, there are "good" ones and "bad" ones.

This is another old-timer of an idea, usually entertained by whites struggling to explain why they are not racists. The mere act of distinguishing between "goodness" and "badness" may seem reasonable. But since when do any of us — other than while making racial or other indefensible judgments — sum up any person as entirely good or bad? I have heard plenty of whites hem and haw about the good and the bad in the black population. But do they commonly talk about good and bad whites? Or Germans? Or Poles? It sounds as if what they really mean is, "I have to approach black people carefully, because a whole lot of them are bad." Suddenly, it's not so reasonable, is it?

5. We've now had two black secretaries of state in a row. How racist can America still be?

Pointing to the rise of Colin Powell and Condoleezza Rice as bellwethers of overall black progress is like pointing to the success of Britney Spears as an example of how well-off white Americans are. Do working whites accept the success of white elites as being a solution to the unaffordable health care and stagnant wages suffered by most whites? Powell (until he bought into the Iraq War) and Rice did well for themselves hitching their stars to the Republican Party. Good for them. What is good for the bulk of black Americans who have continued to suffer under conservative policies, however, is another story entirely.

6. Other immigrants had a hard time, too. What's so different about blacks?

Well, let's list some of the differences:

- Blacks were forcibly enslaved, their languages and cultures forbidden, their families broken up, and legally defined as subhuman and purchasable property for centuries. After slavery, blacks existed under a system of legal apartheid for another hundred years.
- Blacks were subject to lynching and other acts of terror in numbers exponentially greater than even the most hated European immigrants.
- Blacks have never been able to move into the realm of mainstream whiteness, as have European immigrants.
- Blacks remain the object of outright racial discrimination and racial hate crimes, something American whites will never suffer on an equivalent scale.

I could go on. Let's just say that if you're white, this is not a good argument to try to make.

7. I'm afraid to talk with an African American about race. They're too touchy.

Too touchy? In an era when Rage Talkers on TV and radio take for granted a slash-and-burn form of verbal annihilation that would have embarrassed Attila the Hun? Sure, black Americans can be touchy sometimes. So can you. Buck up and stop being a baby. I mean, who came up with the fainthearted idea that blacks and whites will break out in hives when they disagree? I want to find our smilingly unbiased "harmony" consultants and slap them until they confess to having opinions. Slinking off silently does no one any good. And even "touchy" honest dialogue will be a big improvement over the mainstream standard of discourse that Americans have now gotten used to.

8. The existence of black conservatives proves that old-style black liberals can't speak for blacks anymore.

No one group can speak for "blacks." Black conservatives, however, in a prevailing conservative climate, have enjoyed a prominence far out of proportion to their representation of prevailing points of view among blacks. The fact is that polls routinely show the vast majority of blacks in sync with the positions of those "old-style black liberals."

9. There is such a thing as "the black community."

No, there isn't. Look at the layers within the "white community," from elites to middle- and working-class communities to the poor, and you will see the same complexities among American blacks. Factor in regional cultures on top of that, and the infinite varieties of human nature and experience, and you start to get the idea. Reporters sometimes speak of "the black community" because it saves them the trouble of looking at the actual people involved, and even then they usually mean "the poor," which is mere shorthand for another set of complexities. The real questions are: Which black people? Where? With what vested interests and what points of view? And with what disagreements among them? If you're not getting these details, you're not getting the true story.

10. Blacks act as if slavery happened yesterday. They can't let go of it.

This bad idea among some whites just doesn't seem to go away. For a black person caught speeding ninety miles an hour to claim that slavery got him a traffic ticket is one thing. But let's look at the record. Slavery was outlawed in this country less than 150 years ago. Roughly two human beings or ten dogs or one tortoise could live and die in that length of time. The period since legal slavery is just three times since the end of World War II. It is barely twice the age of the American automobile. It is no time at all. When Americans truly let go of the legacy of slavery — that is, when race has no bearing on access to a decent education, career prosperity, or the likelihood of ending up on death row — then black people, too, will forget about slavery. Until then, we can all expect to encounter the aftershocks of slavery daily.

The Ten Most Bigoted Ideas
Held by Black Americans

1. Gay marriage, and gayness in general, are a threat to black communities.

This is the single most odiously bigoted tendency to publicly emerge among significant numbers of black Americans in a long, long time. It is cause for shame both among those black leaders who trumpet its reprehensible claims — including, sadly, a number of black ministers — and among those parishioners and citizens who join in the chorus. Most of its fury is aimed at homosexuality (i.e., male-to-male same-sex relations). The gist of its twisted logic is that homosexuality is not only ungodly but also a threat to strong black manhood. We already know how antigay crusaders like to cherry-pick Bible verses that condemn gays and ignore those verses that do not. But the black antigay grudge goes deeper. What this tantrum is really about is the desperation felt in many poor black communities about the dearth of strong, positive black male role models, since so many black men are in jail, on drugs, or dead in their twenties. America is indeed hell on black men, and the panic over this very real crisis of a strong black male presence has made gay black men an easy scapegoat for angry citizens and easy fodder for religious demagogues looking to make righteous noise. The fact is, however, that strong maleness bears no relation whatsoever to sexual orientation, and homosexuality did not create the joblessness, drugs, and violence that plague poor black neighborhoods. Blacks who spout this homophobic meanness ought to get down on their knees and ask forgiveness, particularly given blacks' own bloody history of struggle for civil and human rights.

2. Hey, at least the post-9/11 anti-Arab hysteria takes some of the heat off of us blacks.

What a stupid, cruel, and self-destructive position to take: condoning the kind of brutality that has hammered you for years by wishing it upon someone else. First of all, the immorality and the astonishing irony of blacks' rationalizing the ethnic mistreatment of others takes the breath away. Second, the self-defeating nature of such logic is excruciatingly obvious: after Arab Americans, what group do you think is next in line for surveillance, possible detention, and free-for-all legal mistreatment by an expanded national security state? Take a guess.

3. White people are just messed up. Look at the racist, right-wing stuff they believe. They're hopeless.

We interrupt this diatribe with some facts: First, whites are far more liberal on the issues than the dominant news and commentary would have you believe. In polls, large percentages of whites support single-payer health care, more money for public schools, and protection of social service programs. It is conservative Rage Talk politics and punditry, and the disproportionate legitimacy both receive in mainstream media coverage, that create the illusion of a huge majority of whites having been suckered by Rush Limbaugh and Bill O'Reilly. Don't believe the hype. Second, if you were white, overworked, underpaid, stressed, angry, and a cable subscriber, you yourself might well swallow the stuff that the Fox watchers take on faith. Don't mistake the nature of centralized media for human nature.

4. Only a white person can be racist.

Here is another misused notion: the idea that black hatred toward whites cannot be racist because it is not based on a history of officially sanctioned and organized oppression.

The kernel of truth here is that American racism, as an *institutionalized system of racial preference,* is in fact a white phenomenon for which there is no black equivalent. But hold on. It's also true that *racial prejudice,* the simple race-based hatred or stereotyping of another, is an equal-opportunity dysfunction that can take up residence in any-one of any color. Worse, it's contagious. Think you're immune because you're black? Think again.

5. In America, it's all about race. Everything else takes a back seat.

Race is huge, no question about it. But if you think race is what drives most American policy, consider this: If all of the private money were taken out of politics, and all local and state and federal political campaigns (including races for the House, the Senate, and the presidency) were pub-licly financed, and anyone was free to win election on the basis of the popular appeal of his or her ideas, America would very likely have a system of affordable health care for all, mega-funded public schools, social supports, jobs programs for the needy, funding for drug treatment on de-mand, and much higher government-mandated wages and benefits for even the lowest-paying jobs. So what do *you* think is the single biggest impediment to more progressive public policy?

6. A black person can never get ahead. Whites have the game rigged too well.

Yeah. That's why Oprah, former NAACP president Kweisi Mfume, Cornel West, Toni Morrison, Maya Angelou,

Henry Louis Gates Jr., Madame C. J. Walker, publishers Earl Graves (*Black Enterprise*) and John H. Johnson (*Ebony*), American Express CEO Kenneth Chenault, world-famous surgeon Dr. Benjamin Carson, Alice Walker, Duke Ellington, John Coltrane, Ella Fitzgerald, Sarah Vaughan, Spike Lee, Denzel Washington, Queen Latifah, and Gordon Parks never made it.

7. Why argue? A white person will never understand.

This little toxin has a long, long half-life. All I'll say is this: It's a free country. Give up if you want to. But who said there was ever going to be total understanding? Who said that the only acceptable outcome of any conversation was complete agreement? In a dialogue between a black person and a white one, maybe neither will ever fully understand the other. But perhaps it's not about the pursuit of some holy grail of total understanding. Perhaps it's about gaining ground in spite of friction. So my question to you is: Are you afraid to stand on your feet and try?

8. White people just don't like black people, period. They never will.

Right. That's why most white suburban kids wish they were black (at least until it's time for them to look for a job) and try their best to act that way. That's why whites have aped virtually every aspect of black American culture for the past hundred years. That's why there are now more interracial marriages than ever, and more biracial children, and why there is more depiction of interracial love on TV and in the movies, and in a gradually more realistic way than before. Wake up and smell the coffee. The problem isn't that most whites inherently dislike like black people. The problem is that many whites — with a lot of help from the news media and Rage Talkers and imbalanced political policy — don't *understand* black people or the situations in which many black people live. And that's an entirely different and much more serious issue.

9. Why should blacks have to push to raise issues? White people started American racism. So they should be the ones to address it.

Sure, and it was the shipbuilder's job to rescue people from the *Titanic*. Let the racists who cling to "unsinkable" white privilege go down with the ship. This water's cold. Learn to swim. And if you want to increase the chances of having some good people survive with you, push others to learn, too.

10. Straight hair is "good" hair. And lighter skin is prettier. And a thinner nose is . . .

What a shame to even have to talk about this in the twenty-first century. But when you can still hear such comments in black beauty parlors, and when *Ebony* is still parading black male celebrities on its cover with their lighter-skinned wives, and when Michael Jackson is . . . well, anyway, you know we still have a distance to go. For sure, having choices, whether in doing different things with your hair or in choosing partners, is all good when it's based on self-liking. Let's just make sure we stay true to that self-liking part.

21

The Color of Love: Interracial Relationships in Black and White

T rue stories:

At a historically black university, there is a screening of the just-released film Something New, a movie in which the protagonist, a gorgeous professional single black woman who imagines her perfect match as a sophisticated black beau, tries to fight off her attraction to a handsome white landscape architect. The two begin to date. Sparks fly, and she eventually allows herself to surrender to her desire. In the university auditorium, at the climactic scene in the film in which the white hunk sweeps the black heroine into bed, the primarily black audience erupts. Some stand, pump their fists, and cheer.

Others boo. This movie is saying something, and some viewers like the message, while others are not so pleased.

In a major city, a black man and a white woman in a sporty car stop at a traffic light. A white man pulls alongside in a pickup truck and locks his eyes on them. He stares at the two of them with such apoplectic rage that they almost expect his brain to burst and blood to spew out from behind his eyes. He grips the wheel and continues to stare, a skinny man of stone, eyes fixed on the white woman and the black man through a long red light. What do they do? They make funny faces at him. They stick out their tongues, waggle their hands behind their ears, laugh. His face reddens. His expression says he might like to kill them, this nigger and Snow White in their sports car. But the light changes. Everyone drives away.

At a cocktail party hosted by friends, a West African woman introduces her white American husband to assorted guests of various nationalities and ethnicities. They all greet her husband warmly, with one obvious exception: the black Americans are cold to the point of rudeness. Later, the embarrassed host apologizes to the couple; some black Americans, the host tells them, seem to have a problem.

Interracial love in a nation that has long been racially at war. What could cut closer to the bone than our choice of those with whom we share flesh? Race is nothing: cultural habits, melanin, accident, physical scenery. Race is everything: slavery, self-love, self-hate. For black and white interracial lovers, whether rich or poor, gay or straight, there is the same procession of scattered strangers who shout into your partnership their message that color counts. More than just public manners are abandoned over this fixation. At its worst, people are beaten up or killed for this, daughters and sons disowned, friends estranged, bitter recriminations flung:

"You'll date *anything* white," says a black woman to a black male friend after meeting his white girlfriend.

"You want that black lovin'," sneers a white man at his younger sister upon hearing that she has a date with a black man.

"You're ugly. They're better-looking," one black woman feels she is being told, without a word being spoken, when she sees a black man date a procession of white women.

"You're a loser. They're winners," one black man feels he is being told, with no words spoken, when he sees a black woman dating a white man.

Let us not act surprised. With weapons stuffed in every nook and cranny of America's shared racial house, why should our bedroom be safe? Sex is the most potent expression of personal power we have. It is no accident that once upon a time in America, sweaty white men hacked off black penises and testicles while white women watched, or that, today, young men on street corners still clutch their own family jewels. Still, the emotional abattoir that our country's history has made of interracial love and kisses — or even the rumor of them — nearly defies description. The legacy in broken hearts and bones, not to mention bruised feelings at parties and on dinner dates, is more than we can know.

The good news is that things are not what they used to

be. In fact, on some fronts the dynamic of interracial love is changing with almost, well, color-blinding speed. There were about 150,000 interracial married couples in America in 1960; by 2000, there were 1.46 million. Of those, black/white married interracial couples increased from 51,000 in 1960 to 363,000 in 2000, more than tripling as a percentage of all married couples.[1] In movies, TV sitcoms, and dramatic series within the past decade alone, interracial relationships, including those between blacks and whites, have gone from being rare and cautiously presented to being fairly common and casually regarded. The TV shows *Sex and the City, Supernatural, Grey's Anatomy, Lost, My Name Is Earl, Veronica Mars, Six Feet Under* and *ER* have all included interracial or cross-cultural romances, and not all of the black/white couplings have followed the old formula of black men bedding white women. *Supernatural,* for instance, had a romance between a black female and a white male character. *Six Feet Under* had a subplot involving gay male characters, one white and one black. And in the aforementioned movie *Something New,* the black female protagonist is not only beautiful and educated, but is also the apple of the handsome white leading man's eye — a long-overdue turnabout of Hollywood racial convention that accounts for some of the cultural waves, and raves, generated by the film.

There were also boos in the auditorium, however, during *Something New.* To be sure, there is nothing new about the sometimes less-than-jubilant reactions to interracial love, particularly love between black and white Americans, who share a uniquely and potently eroticized history. If you are black or if you are white, it's an issue that has likely in some way affected your own personal history.

When I was a teenager, I was briefly sweet on a white girl I'll call Carol. She was smart and cute. She liked me and I liked her. We went on a couple of dates, held hands, talked on the phone, felt warm inside. Then, one day, she wouldn't talk to me, wouldn't see me. Without explanation, it was over. I was as heartbroken as a teenager can manage to be. We both graduated from high school without speaking of it again. But years later I saw Carol at a high school reunion, and I asked her why she had dumped me. She told me, through a tight throat, that she had been beaten by her grandfather and forbidden to ever see "that nigger" again.

I tell you this story not because there is anything special about it, but because there is not. Even today, with interracial relationships more visible than ever, it happens all the time. And it is about much more than whites simply "not liking" blacks, or vice versa. There is a nuclear-powered mythology that fuels our sexual racism, and it has blacks and whites bursting out of their skins to get at each other, sometimes with sex on their minds, sometimes with murder.

Why? Where does this lust/hate come from? And, whether you are dating interracially or watching from the sidelines, how do you avoid becoming a casualty of society's passions?

Beneath It All

Let's start with what might be our nation's deepest-running sexual neurosis: the age-old fascination with what goes on between black men and white women. The specter of marauding black men ravaging fair white women held spellbound by sexual magnetism is an American article of faith. It was (and is) the obsession behind the compulsive lynching of black men, for which the alleged rape of white women has nearly always been offered as explanation. It is also the reason why, for so long, many movies and TV dramas about interracial romance portrayed simplistic, doomed trysts between virile black men and naive white women.

For example, *The Affair,* a 1995 made-for-cable movie, featured a dashing young black soldier stationed in England who tumbled into a torrid romance with the sheltered white wife of a passionless bureaucrat. They were found out; she was coerced into claiming rape; he was hanged; she was forever heartbroken. The message — interracial love is irresistible poison — has been a longtime theme in American novels and films, although, thankfully, nowhere near as pervasive today as in the days of such bodice-rippers as the slavery-themed *Mandingo.* Like the early American captivity narratives in which white women were abducted by Native Americans, this fable of black man/white woman relationships became cherished social text, despite countervailing evidence of healthy interracial love.

Why the erotic fairy tales? Because America's Puritan-influenced culture, preoccupied as it is with the bogeyman of sex, eroticized the very idea of blackness by defining blacks as primitives. This served, early on, to justify slavery; the stereotype of black savagery was popularly embraced as the antithesis of the alleged dignity (and sexual restraint) of white life.

But gender mattered, too. As Cornel West has said in *Race Matters,*[2] because ours is a sex-obsessed society in which men are expected to be the more sexually aggressive, the "primitive" stereotype heightened the sexual appeal of black men to whites, while demeaning the sexual appeal of black women (at least in public). The mantle of delicate and refined femininity fell instead to white women, in the form of a stereotype of white female sex appeal. To be sure, this "favored" sexual stature has been no picnic for either black men or white women. Black men, as part of the bargain of being sexually glorified, remain the most reviled (and disproportionately imprisoned) men in America. And white women find themselves held to an impossible duality of goddess/whore femininity, while also facing the universal problems of sexual discrimination, abuse, and violence.

Still, it all sets the stage for today's occasional hateful stares at black male/white female couples. The myth demeans everyone. Many black women, seeing this game for what it is (and seeing many black men play along), have grown bitterly resentful of having been left in the lurch. And many white men, simultaneously awed and threatened by the sexual hype about black men, seethe when they see "their" women "deserting" them for supposedly greener sexual pastures. Anger? Yes, and plenty of it.

Any African-American woman with dark skin, full lips, and kinky hair knows how it feels to have her beauty shunted aside in favor of the white version: light skin, straight hair, blue or green or gray eyes, and so on. Worse yet, black women have seen droves of African-American men buy into the notions that white women are prettier and that black men are more potent. It is as if legions of African-American men, over the centuries, have been willing to strike a nasty deal with white Americans: *I'll let you despise me if you'll sexually desire me.* In the bargain, a great many black men and black women have come to accept the idea that the whiter-looking you are, the more attractive you are. Only a generation ago, it was common to hear black men boast to one another about having found a white woman or a "high-yellow" (light-skinned) black woman. My mother remembers hearing black men of her generation, mocked for dating homely white women, snap back, "Well, at least she's white."

The attitude persists among some black American men even today. One black female friend of mine, whenever she hears through the grapevine that some black man is dating a white woman, likes to ask sarcastically, "Which is she, overweight or ugly?" The tendency, my friend insists — with some serious topspin on her attitude — is for black men and less attractive white women to "settle" for each other: he wants a white woman, she wants a man who will accept her. It is an image that provokes instant ire among many blacks, particularly women. When an interracial couple appears to fit this description, one can witness a trail of disdainful glances in their wake. As to how often this dynamic actually plays out in relationships, who of us is in a position to know with certainty, given the sensitivity of many of us to even the hint of it? But we know it happens. As does, under similar social pressures, the phenomenon of some black men "dating downward" in economic class in order to find white women who will accept them.

As if all of this were not enough, consider the terrible toll that poverty, prison, and drugs take on today's population of eligible African-American males. It is easy to understand the narrowing of options felt by many black women, particularly single and educated black women. For some, the mere sight of a black man with a white woman becomes, rightly or wrongly, a jabbing symbol of black men succumbing to the influence of white values. It hurts. This is where the glares, and the cutting of eyes, come from.

Certain white men also see red at the prospect of any turn-on between black men and white women, although such injury is pretty much limited to matters of ego. After all, white men still own more property, wield more political power, enjoy more social respect, and can date and marry among a broad range of women if they choose. To the extent that they are victims, it is from buying into the "jungle brute" stereotype of blacks, thereby dooming themselves to feeling like sexual wimps in comparison. Bet on it: when such a white man scowls at a black man and a white woman, his pain originates somewhere in the groin.

The same sexual-animal mythology can play out in how relationships between black women and white men are perceived. After all, whites applied the sex-hungry stereotype to black women as well, creating a "savage" fantasy parallel to that of black men. And this Puritan-based white caricature of the untamed black woman was accompanied by the desire to get naked with her. On the plantation, white men embraced one version of the feminine ideal in public, and another in private — often by force. Rape of black female slaves and servants was common and brutal. And the sexual dynamic between white master and female slave created its own world of super-charged symbolic roles: the white master as a figure who could bestow favor upon a sexually compliant black woman; the black man as a potential loser to the white man in the realm of being a "provider." With the diminished expectations by black women (who often headed slave households) of the power of black men, and the emasculating sense of despair felt by black men at their own perceived diminishment, the potential for relationships between black women and white men left a legacy of tension and mistrust.

And so a relationship between a black woman and a white man can evoke for some — and perhaps for themselves — stubborn historical stereotypes. Black men may sneer (though at great risk of hypocrisy) at the couple like spurned suitors, wondering to themselves what privilege the black woman is getting from her white mate. Maybe you remember, for example, the adjustment required of some black men in the 1980s when the media latched onto the story of upwardly mobile black women exercising their option to date white professional men. The angle played up in many of the stories — a sensational one, but fair — could be summed up as "What's good for the goose is good for the gander." In other words, if black men can date whites, so can black women. Some white women, for their part, suck their teeth at white male/black female couples, as if in disdain of a white man's falling for what they assume to be the primal power and sexual abandon of a black woman. And blacks and whites alike may flinch, even today, at the surprise of seeing, in public, an apparent rejection of cherished white female standards of beauty.

All of this, of course, goes deeper than gender or sexual preference. Whether straight, gay, lesbian, or bisexual, relationships involving black and white partners touch on nerves. They call up, inevitably, all manner of venerable stereotypes involving black men and black women and white women and white men. Insecurity, hypocrisy, prejudice, power: the whole conflagration trailing us, in the streets and bedrooms of America, like noisy shadows. How do lovers find peace in such a place?

Dealing with It

So you love someone who is white. Or someone who is black. And other people, crouched in various spots along your path, feel free to think their narrow-minded thoughts and fling their coded little accusations:

"You're a black stud on a white leash."

"You're a white woman who craves black meat."

"You're a black woman out for a white sugar daddy."

"You're an Uncle Tom who'll take anybody who's white."

"You're a black person with low self-esteem."

"You're a white person who's out to make a statement."

"You're desperate."

"You're pathetic."

All of which beg the question: Are you? Do you actually believe that white women are better-looking than black women? Do you presume to have no use for black men, and consider white men more attractive prospects? Do you seek, in black men or women, a bestial savagery your race lacks? They are fair questions. You ought to answer them. To yourself. To your satisfaction. Do you know who you are, where you come from, what heritage you own? Do you respect your own background and origins, and those of your partner? Do you find your lover's humanity to be more engaging than his skin color or his sexuality or her hair? Nobody can answer these questions but you. And, as an American raised on race like the rest of us, you had better answer them honestly if you expect anything close to inner peace in our color-conscious society.

Look in the mirror. Look at how you treat your own ethnicity. Look at your patterns in choosing partners, if you can recognize any. Look at your partner's view of your ethnicity. See any changes that you need to make in yourself or your relationship? Make them. Feel any discomfort with who you are? Address it. Only when you have been willing to stare at yourself will you be able hold on to your true identity in the face of others' spiteful stereotypes. Only when you have locked eyes with yourself will you become less vulnerable, on the street or at your parents' Thanksgiving dinner, to other people's potentially harsh judgment of your choice of partners.

It is important, I think, for people who date interracially to understand the source of certain kinds of resentment without surrendering to it. The anger with which black women sometimes regard black male/white female relationships, for example, deserves to be taken seriously. This is no matter of petty jealousy. It is a naturally fierce reaction to the historical attack against black femininity — an attack in which some black men, to their collective discredit, have been accomplices by flocking to the Marilyn Monroe side of the theater in pursuit of white norms of femininity. The shame is not strictly one-sided; "white-is-right" values have also influenced black women, as in, for example, the longtime (but hopefully fading) popularity of alleged skin-lightening creams. The notion that kinky black hair *had* to be artificially straightened (as opposed to this being an uncoerced matter of fashion choice, as many black women now see it) and the labeling

of naturally straight (Caucasian) hair as "good" hair re-
flected self-contempt among both black men and black
women.

But the fact remains that while black women found
themselves facing cosmetic rejection, some black men reinforced that very rejection through an explicit preference
for white standards of beauty — for three-hundred-some-
odd years. I'd call that a long insult. It would behoove
you, if you are a black man, or if you are a white woman
who loves a black man, to have some empathy for the resulting pain and anger on the part of African-American
women. When black women give that stare, you should
understand the source but reject the judgment. Respond, if
you choose to, by looking back at them with a mixture of
understanding and resolve. If, as a couple, you have built a
relationship with respect for yourselves and your cultures,
you have no explaining to do.

If you are a black woman with a white man, you
don't owe black men any explanations, either, particularly
given the history of black men in interracial romance. But
you, too, can try to carry yourself with an understanding
of the pain shared by black women and black men. The
shared history of black American women and men has left
deeply bruised spots on the souls of both. Neither is un-
scarred. In America's four-century interracial tryst, black
women and black men have suffered the most harm. Both
need to heal.

And what if you are someone on the outside glaring
in, who disapproves of many, or all, interracial relationships? Well, if you are able to reason, you need to know
that your angry sizing-up of interracial relationships is
nowhere near as accurate as you think it is. Your own sen-

sitivities get in your way. You scrutinize couples for the glaring signs — educated black person dating down, white person out for dark thrills, black person who has given up on dating blacks — and you think you find your proof. But the truth is that much of the time, you cannot even begin to tell by looking. There is simply too much that you do not know about both people, too much anger and too little information. And if you do happen to correctly diagnose one couple's dysfunction on a street corner, is it worth having flung unjustified fury in the faces of so many others? I can't see how.

Even if you are acquainted with a person and disapprove of his or her black or white partner, your opinion is worth no more than the experience it is etched on. But when you make snap judgments of strangers, in public, based solely on the film loops in your own mind, you commit a worse offense: you are dumping your garbage into the personal space of perfect strangers.

I know: If you are an African-American woman, in particular, it might be hard to not feel your jaw tighten when you see a black man hand-in-hand with a white woman. You know the damage done by the widely held black stud/white princess fantasy; the decades of racial indoctrination; the skin bleaching creams and corrosive hair-straightening compounds and hot combs; the little black girls who drape shirts from their heads, tossing the fabric in imitation of long, straight hair; the black men who lose their minds to the Hollywood blond factory.

But think about this: If you happened to meet a white man, and to feel attracted to him, and to proceed to build, to your mutual delight, a loving relationship founded on personal and cultural respect and compatibility, how would you then feel if utter strangers sucked their teeth at the two of you? And made you objects of public scorn at random intervals?

Some black men and white women may date for the wrong reasons. And some date for the right ones. People of every color and nationality date for what you and I might view as right and wrong reasons, or combinations of the two. It seems to me that those couples who have, in fact, managed to swim above racist stereotype do not deserve your glares. They deserve your respect. And on a street corner or in a restaurant, you cannot tell which interracial couple is which.

Wouldn't it be better to be angry, if at all, at situations about which you knew the details, and in which you could accomplish something through true communication? If your brother or sister or close friend continually dates in a way that appears to use race destructively — as a way to get at one's family or seek exotic thrills or compensate for insecurities — then maybe the two of you can talk. Maybe. But barring any such personal credentials, your aiming corrective commentary — verbally or nonverbally — at interracial couples is way out of line.

If, on the other hand, you are a black or white American who is just dead set against any white and black touching of the skin, what can I tell you? Take a deep breath. Take your heart pills. African Americans are not shipping out, and neither are whites, and the longer we share a nation, the more of us there will be who feel mutually attracted and who decide to do something about it. This cross-flowering of humanity is happening, and growing, all around you: in relationships, in marriages, in family life, and even on TV and in the movies. It is miraculous, in its way, that in spite of centuries of slogging through stereotype, happy black/white couples insist on happening. They are a triumph over a history of war. The interracial couple at the next table, about whom you are prepared to whisper unkindly, may have a far more fulfilling relationship than you and your own mate.

Early in our history, America turned interracial love — the simple act of love between people of different colors and heritages — into Interracial Love: an epic of lust, slaughter, cultural betrayal, and reconciliation. But, with the inevitability of forward motion and the undeniable knowledge of the heart, we Americans are reclaiming lower-case interracial love, real-life love as it happens between black and white people who want to eat and to dance, who want to help build neighborhoods, who want to raise children who will carry our cultures forward together.

So tell me: what's not to like about love?

Survival Suggestions

1. You be the judge of your relationship.

If you get flak from others about your relationship, realize that their glares and aggravation are just that: theirs. If there are questions about your relationship — and maybe there are — you need to be the one to ask them, whether about yourself or your partner. Dating across races or cultures is only one of countless ways of bridging experiences through romance. But it just so happens, because of our nation's peculiar history, that black/white romance is one of the realms of love that Americans feel most moved to observe and judge. Such judgments may or may not be an issue for your family or friends. But the only judgment for you to accept is your own. If your love is good, hold on to it and savor it. And let others suck on their own bitterness if they so choose. If you come under hostile scrutiny — say, in a restaurant — ignoring the offending parties is usually best. In rare and very confrontational situations, you may feel the need to react. But in general, your undisturbed happiness with your partner is the best reply to a disapproving stranger.

2. Don't dump your racial baggage onto interracial couples.

If you're acting out your own bigotry, it's just plain mean as well as dysfunctional on your part. And if you're reacting to what you see as racial dysfunction, it's still mean — and it's not nearly as well informed as you think. Admit it: You don't know anywhere near as much as you think you do about other people's romances, especially those of strangers. Your unkindness is an unforgivable mistreatment of people whose reasons for being together transcend your knowledge. And even if you happen to guess right about some aspect of their attraction of which you disapprove, what gives you the right to be mean about it? Treat others as you would want to be treated. And point your anger in a direction where it can do some good, such as working to reduce racial stereotypes in the first place.

Epilogue: Is There Hope?

S ome years ago, at the conclusion of one of my talks, a young woman rose and asked me a question I will never forget.

"Your hope that we can make things better sounds great," she said. "But do you really believe that will happen? Do you really think Americans can undo all this damage? Doesn't it ever look hopeless to you? Don't you ever get depressed about it?"

What I told her then is what I will tell you now.

I certainly do get depressed. Seeing my nation's leadership twist the message of September 11 into an agenda that has heightened hatred, ethnically scapegoated innocent people, killed tens of thousands, and further endangered us all has brought me to dismay almost beyond words. Witnessing the rise of a theatrically enraged talk show culture that obscures the issues of greatest meaning to Americans of all colors has left me feeling, at times, downright mournful. Seeing Americans of different ethnicities and religions and sexual orientations pitted against one another while our national treasury is pillaged against our shared interests is more painful to me than you can imagine.

Yes, I get depressed. I have days when I wonder if we, as Americans, can and will rise to the occasion of what is demanded of us.

But to me, the question is not how we can be sure that fairness will win in the end. The question is not how we can know for certain that we will one day have a society in which our politics is driven by the best in us instead of being manipulated by appeals to the worst in us. The question is not how we can feel absolutely assured that fairness will one day prevail. The question is not how to gain a guarantee that we will succeed in making this society a better one.

To me, the question, the one and only question, is:

Are we willing to try?

Acknowledgments

My thanks to Mary Clare Rietz, a friend and comrade who along with Ward Ensign is doing the kind of work that needs to be done everywhere. Her commitment to human goodness is an inspiration to me. My thanks as well to Sondra Thiederman, Ph.D., whose support and perspective are valuable beyond words. Thank you to Norine Dresser for her generosity and camaraderie over the years. Thanks also to Dave Parlett, whose technical expertise has saved me more than once; to Ruth Galer, whose typing was a godsend; and to Fred Mueller, who provided the author photograph. Thanks to all those who provided, or steered me toward, information and resources that I needed. Perpetual thanks to my literary agents, Sheree Bykofsky and Janet Rosen, who have been there for me every step of the way. And finally, I thank my family, who provided the foundation for what I believe and what I try to accomplish with this book.

Baltimore, Maryland
October 2006

Recommended Resources

Appiah, Kwame Anthony, and Henry Louis Gates Jr., eds. *The Dictionary of Global Culture*. New York: Alfred A. Knopf, 1997.

Barber, Benjamin. *Jihad vs. McWorld: How Globalism and Tribalism Are Reshaping the World*. New York: Ballantine Books, 1996.

Berger, Maurice. *White Lies: Race and the Myths of Whiteness*. New York: Farrar, Straus & Giroux, 1999.

Brown, Claude. *Manchild in the Promised Land*. 1965; reprint, New York: Touchstone, 1999.

Chang, Jeff. *Can't Stop Won't Stop: A History of the Hip-Hop Generation*. New York: St. Martin's Press, 2005.

Dahmash-jarrah, Samar. *Arab Voices Speak to American Hearts*. New York: Olive Branch Press, 2005.

de Becker, Gavin. *Fear Less: Real Truth about Risk, Safety, and Security in a Time of Terrorism*. Boston: Little, Brown, 2002.

———. *The Gift of Fear: Survival Signals That Protect Us from Violence*. Boston: Little, Brown, 1997.

Dresser, Norine. *Multicultural Manners: Essential Rules of Etiquette for the 21st Century*. Rev. ed. New York: John Wiley & Sons, 2005.

Dyson, Michael Eric. *Come Hell or High Water: Hurricane Katrina and the Color of Disaster.* Perseus Books, 2006.

———. *Is Bill Cosby Right? Or Has the Black Middle Class Lost Its Mind?* New York: Basic Civitas Books, 2005.

Everett, Percival. *Erasure.* Hanover, N.H.: University Press of New England, 2001.

Frank, Thomas. *What's the Matter with Kansas? How Conservatives Won the Heart of America.* New York: Metropolitan Books, 2004.

Graham, Lawrence Otis. *Member of the Club: Reflections on Life in a Racially Polarized World.* New York: Harper-Collins, 1995.

Griffin, John Howard. *Black Like Me.* 1960; reprint, New York: NAL Trade, 2003.

Guralnick, Peter. *Last Train to Memphis: The Rise of Elvis Presley.* Boston: Little, Brown,1994.

Hart, Peter, for Fairness and Accuracy in Reporting (FAIR). *The Oh, Really? Factor: Unspinning Fox News Channel's Bill O'Reilly.* New York: Seven Stories Press, 2003.

Herman, Edward S., and Noam Chomsky. *Manufacturing Consent: The Political Economy of the Mass Media.* New York: Pantheon, 2002.

hooks, bell. *Outlaw Culture: Resisting Representations.* New York: Routledge, 1994.

Jones, LeRoi (Amiri Baraka). *Blues People: Negro Music in White America.* 1963; reprint, New York: HarperPerennial, 1999.

Katznelson, Ira. *When Affirmative Action Was White: An Untold History of Racial Inequality in Twentieth-Century America.* New York: W.W. Norton, 2005.

Kayyali, Randa A. *The Arab Americans (The New Americans).* Westport, Conn.: Greenwood Press, 2005.

Kelley, Robin D. G. *Yo' Mama's Disfunktional! Fighting the Culture Wars in Urban America.* Boston: Beacon, 1997.

Kitwana, Bakari. *Why White Kids Love Hip Hop: Wangstas, Wig-

gers, Wannabes, and the New Reality of Race in America. New York: Basic Civitas Books, 2005.

Lee, Spike. *When the Levees Broke: A Requiem in Four Acts.* HBO, August 2006.

Massaquoi, Hans J. *Destined to Witness: Growing Up Black in Nazi Germany.* New York: HarperPerennial, 2001.

McCall, Nathan. *Makes Me Wanna Holler: A Young Black Man in America.* New York: Vintage, 1995.

McChesney, Robert W. *The Problem of the Media: U.S. Communication Politics in the 21st Century.* New York: Monthly Review Press, 2004.

Miller, Mark Crispin. *Boxed In: The Culture of TV.* Evanston, Ill.: Northwestern University Press, 1988.

— — —. *The Bush Dyslexicon: Observations on a National Disorder.* New York: W. W. Norton, 2002.

Moore, Michael. *Stupid White Men . . . and Other Sorry Excuses for the State of the Nation!* New York: Regan Books, 2002.

Myers, Jim. *Afraid of the Dark: What Whites and Blacks Need to Know about Each Other.* Chicago: Lawrence Hill Books, 2000.

Rendall, Steven, Jim Naureckas, and Jeff Cohen, for Fairness and Accuracy in Reporting (FAIR). *The Way Things Aren't: Rush Limbaugh's Reign of Error.* New York: New Press, 1995.

Roediger, David R. *Working toward Whiteness: How America's Immigrants Became White.* New York: Basic Books, 2005.

Steele, Shelby. *The Content of Our Character: A New Vision of Race in America.* New York: HarperPerennial, 1991.

Tate, Greg, ed. *Everything but the Burden: What White People Are Taking from Black Culture.* New York: Harlem Moon, 2003.

Tate, Greg. *Flyboy in the Buttermilk: Essays on Contemporary America.* New York: Simon & Schuster, 1992.

Tatum, Beverly Daniel. *"Why Are All the Black Kids Sitting Together in the Cafeteria?": A Psychologist Explains the*

Development of Racial Identity. Rev. ed. New York: Basic Books, 2003.

Thiederman, Sondra, Ph.D. *Making Diversity Work: 7 Steps for Defeating Bias in the Workplace.* Chicago: Dearborn, 2003.

Watkins, S. Craig. *Hip Hop Matters: Politics, Popular Culture, and the Struggle for the Soul of a Movement.* Boston: Beacon Press, 2005.

West, Cornel. *Race Matters.* Boston: Beacon, 1993.

Notes

CHAPTER 1   BLACK, WHITE, AND SCARED:
A NEW SCAPEGOATING IN THE POST-9/11 AGE

1. Ann Coulter, *National Review Online,* September 12, 2001.
2. United Nations Development Program, *Human Development Report 1998 Overview.*
3. PersonalBest.com, *Health in America: Putting the Risk of Terrorism in Perspective,* December 19, 2001.

CHAPTER 2   TRAVELING IN TERROR:
SELF-PROTECTION VERSUS EXCESS BAGGAGE

1. Gavin de Becker, *Fear Less: Real Truth about Risk, Safety, and Security in a Time of Terrorism* (Boston: Little, Brown, 2002), 18–19.
2. To cite two examples of many: "Inspection of Air Cargo Perilously Thin in Newark," *Voices of September 11th,* November 17, 2004; "Airport-Security System in U.S. Riddled with Failures," *Seattle Times,* July 13, 2004.
3. Gavin de Becker, *The Gift of Fear: Survival Signals That Protect Us from Violence* (Boston: Little, Brown, 1997).

CHAPTER 3   STILL CAUGHT IN KATRINA:
FACING OUR ONGOING STORM OF RACE AND CLASS

1. "Mayor to Feds: 'Get Off Your Asses,'" CNN.com, September 2, 2005.

2. "White House Knew of Levee's Failure on Night of Storm," *New York Times,* February 10, 2006.

3. "Katrina Aid Far from Flowing," *Los Angeles Times*, August 27, 2006; "'Breathtaking' Waste and Fraud in Hurricane Aid," *New York Times*, June 27, 2006.

4. "Racism, the Media, and Katrina," *Extra!* (magazine of Fairness and Accuracy in Reporting, or FAIR), December 2005.

5. "Year after Katrina, Bush Still Fights for 9/11 Image," *New York Times*, August 27, 2006

6. "Hurricane Katrina Death Toll by Locality," *Wikipedia*, August 2006; "Deaths of Evacuees Push Toll to 1,577," *New Orleans Times-Picayune*, May 19, 2006.

7. "Grassroots Gumbo," *The Nation*, September 18, 2006.

8. "Special Edition of the Katrina Index: A One-Year Review of Key Indicators of Recovery in Post-Storm New Orleans," Brookings Institution, August 2006.

9. "Economic Effects of Hurricane Katrina," *Wikipedia*, September 2006.

10. "Wave of Debt Sweeps Over New Orleans," *USA Today*, May 17, 2006.

CHAPTER 4   SURVIVAL AND STEREOTYPE ON THE STREET

1. "Study: 1 in 5 Young Black City Men in Jail," *Baltimore Sun,* March 16, 2005.

CHAPTER 6   RAGE RADIO AND SCREAMING HEADS:
HOW TO SURVIVE TALK SHOW CULTURE

1. Rush Limbaugh, *Rush Limbaugh Radio Show*, April 29, 1994.

2. Among others, the books include FAIR's *The Way Things*

Aren't: Rush Limbaugh's Reign of Error (New York: New Press, 1995), Al Franken's *Lies and the Lying Liars Who Tell Them: A Fair and Balanced Look at the Right* (New York: Dutton, 2003), and FAIR's *The Oh, Really? Factor: Unspinning Fox News Channel's Bill O'Reilly* (New York: Seven Stories Press, 2003). Web pages that take on the task of rebutting false claims by talk show hosts include Spinsanity.com, Dailyhowler.com, and Mediamatters.org.

3. Program on International Policy Attitudes, University of Maryland, *Misperceptions, the Media and the Iraq War,* October 2, 2003.

4. Ann Coulter, in her syndicated column, December 21, 2005, cited on Mediamatters.org, December 21, 2005.

5. "100 Most Important Talk Show Hosts in America," *Talkers Magazine,* February 2006.

6. Garrison Keillor, "Confessions of a Listener," *Nation,* May 23, 2005.

CHAPTER 8   TILL O. J. DO US PART:
RACE AND OUR ENCOUNTERS WITH POLICE

1. *Race, Rights and Police Brutality,* Amnesty International, September 1, 1999.

2. *Driving while Black: Racial Profiling on Our Nation's Highways,* ACLU, June 7, 1999.

3. Ibid.

4. Ibid.

5. "Know Your Rights: What to Do If You're Stopped by the Police," ACLU.org, July 14, 2004.

CHAPTER 10   AFFIRMATIVE ACTION AND BEYOND:
CONTROVERSIE KATRINA AND THE POOR, THAT WILL NOT
DIE, AND WHY

1. Bill O'Reilly, "Katrina and the Poor," *Fort Lauderdale Sun-*

Sentinel, September 8, 2005, cited in FAIR, *Extra!* November–December 2005, 13.

2. Ira Katznelson, *When Affirmative Action Was White* (New York: W. W. Norton, 2005), 23.

CHAPTER 11   SHOWING OUR ID:
WHAT IS RACE, ANYWAY?

1. For a revealing discussion of this, I suggest David R. Roediger's *Working toward Whiteness: How America's Immigrants Became White* (New York: Basic Books, 2005).

CHAPTER 12   YOU MY NIGGA:
WHO'S NAMING WHOM?

1. Thomas A. Guglielmo, *White on Arrival: Italians, Race, Color, and Power in Chicago, 1890–1945* (New York: Oxford, 2003).

CHAPTER 14   ELVIS TO EMINEM:
BLACK MUSIC AND THE FIGHT OVER WHO OWNS CULTURE

1. Peter Guralnick, *Last Train to Memphis* (Boston: Little, Brown, 1994).
2. Ibid.
3. Mark Crispin Miller, *Boxed In: The Culture of TV* (Evanston, Ill.: Northwestern University Press, 1988).
4. Carl Hancock Rux, "Eminem: The New White Negro," in Greg Tate, ed., *Everything but the Burden* (New York: Harlem Moon, 2003).

CHAPTER 15   HEY, YO: WHAT COLOR DO YOU SPEAK?

1. Zora Neale Hurston, *Their Eyes Were Watching God* (Chicago: University of Illinois Press, 1978), 17, 18.

CHAPTER 21   THE COLOR OF LOVE:
INTERRACIAL RELATIONSHIPS IN BLACK AND WHITE

1. Joint Center for Political and Economic Studies, *Marriage and African Americans,* October 2001.

2. Cornel West, *Race Matters* (Boston: Beacon Press, 1993), 86–90.